CONTINENTAL DRIFT

CONTINENTAL DRIFT

ROBERT BERGEVIN

The lives of the characters are complemented by music. For an enhanced experience, you can get a glimpse of that atmosphere using this QR code:

Illustrations (cover and interior) Mathew Valle - mvvartworks
Cover: Scarlett Ecoffet

Sources for the literary works cited in the novel can be found at the end of the book.

Paper ISBN: 978-2-9822072-4-0
Legal deposit: 1st trimester 2024

To my father,
whom I miss dearly.

PROLOGUE

Every family has its story.

Every story is a myth.

Myths are populated with heroic, divine, and
supernatural characters.

In Jean-Philippe's family, this is the case…

1.

A RUMOR RUNNING AROUND

March 2010

In the cool London spring, Jean-Philippe's bedroom vividly reveals the passion of the past few hours. Naked, with his blankets pushed down to the foot of the bed, he preserves his warmth by keeping his head on Rahim's chest, his hand on his stomach, his legs entwined with those of his lover. Rahim seems to have emerged from a Botticelli painting, with one hand resting on Jean-Philippe's back and the other on his shoulder. Jean-Philippe enjoys Rahim's mellow body and the fuzziness of his chest, comforting him as he sails peacefully in the arms of Morpheus. The double bed, too small for the two grown men, forces them to snuggle up.

Yet when he sleeps at Rahim's condo, Jean-Philippe criticizes his king-size bed as a waste of space, since both of them always share the same half of the mattress. Maybe a double bed isn't a bad idea after all.

Jean-Philippe's phone vibrates on the bedside table, once, twice, three times before Rahim taps his beloved on the shoulder to wake him up.

"JP, it's your mother," Rahim says between breaths.

Jean-Philippe turns over with a groan. The separation of their two bodies is another reason for his discontent.

His mother is the only one who calls like this in the middle of the night. She still doesn't understand the time zone system. She calls from Quebec in the evening, not realizing that it's nighttime in England. Jean-Philippe created a checklist and conversion chart to help her get used to the time difference, but to no avail. After a few futile attempts at trying to explain, he let it go. Once a month, he resolves to cut short his sleep to check on his mother and the family. His eyes still cloudy, he picks up his iPhone.

"Phil, it's Mom! Am I disturbing you?"

"It's okay, I'm awake."

"I-I'm sorry."

Jean-Philippe puts his glasses on and tries to focus on the time displayed on the alarm clock. As he mentally calculates the time difference, a doubt creeps into his mind. His mother usually calls around two o'clock, and it's almost six in the morning.

"It's late at home. Is something wrong?" he asks.

His mother is crying softly on the other end of the line. Jean-Philippe sits up at the foot of the bed.

Rahim takes the opportunity to put his boxers back on and walks to the bathroom.

"Oh, I'm all worked up. I'm running around like crazy."

"What's going on with you? Why are you so emotional?"

"We went to the hospital this afternoon for your father. He fell off the ladder and fainted."

"Did he injure himself?"

"Yes. I mean, I thought he'd broken an arm, but it wasn't that. He sprained his ankle and hurt his knee. The paramedic put a cervical collar on him as a precaution. I don't think anything's broken."

"That's a good thing, isn't it?" says Jean-Philippe, his heart pounding while he keeps a reassuring tone in his voice. "They're still going to check for a concussion, aren't they? They're going to do some tests on him at the hospital, right?"

"Your father said his stomach hurt. He couldn't hold onto the ladder anymore, and that's why he fell. I kept telling him he was overdoing it too, but he wouldn't listen to me! Anyway, the doctors gave him some painkillers and they're going to keep him under observation tomorrow. It's not normal to have such a stomachache that it makes you fall off a ladder! Am I wrong?"

"You were right to call me. I imagine they're going to take some blood samples or X-rays."

"That's what I think too. All week, he had trouble digesting his meals. He was taking antacids, but they didn't help. I thought it was his ulcers coming back. He told the doctor it was like a cramp in the lower abdomen. It was never this bad before."

Rahim replaces the bedspread before lying down, watching his naked boyfriend chat with his mother. Rahim learned some French at school, but he can't follow a discussion between Jean-Philippe and his family, especially in that Quebec French dialect. He takes the opportunity to admire his lover's body, the muscular back and round buttocks he loves so much. He finally closes his eyes, waiting for Jean-Philippe to resume his place in the hollow of his shoulder.

"Your brother's going early tomorrow morning and I'll join him later," Jean-Philippe's mother continues. "Your father got scared and kept repeating your name. He said, 'I want to see Jean-Philippe! I don't want to die,' before losing consciousness. Ah, you know how these things get on my nerves!"

Hearing his father's words, Jean-Philippe feels his heart quicken, like a jolt of adrenalin or a rude awakening.

"Try to get some sleep, Mom. I know it's not easy. If you want to be in shape for Dad tomorrow, you don't have a choice. I'm leaving for Northern Ireland later today, but I'll have my phone with me. If I'm on the plane, leave me a message, and I'll call you as soon as I land. Keep me posted and call me back, okay?"

He ends the call and puts his iPhone back on the table. Rahim takes Jean-Philippe by the waist and pulls him toward him. He drops onto his back and rests his head on Rahim's belly.

Since he, her youngest son, left Quebec five years ago, Jean-Philippe's mother has never missed her monthly check-in. She gives him family news and gossip from his native Ithaca-on-the-Lake.

"What's the news? Who's pregnant this time?" teases Rahim.

"My dad's in the hospital."

His smile fades. "Oh, I'm sorry. I didn't mean to be insensitive."

"Don't worry. I know you don't think bad of anyone," Jean-Philippe reassures him.

He moves up and settles back to lie on Rahim's voluptuous body. He puts his head on Rahim's shoulder, held up by his lover's arms. They wrap themselves beneath the blanket, creating a cocoon of softness, leaving their worries outside.

"What are you going to do?" asks Rahim.

"I'm going to kiss you." He encases his boyfriend's head in his arms and presses his lips to Rahim's.

"Hmm! That wasn't my question, but I'm satisfied with the answer," Rahim says, begging for another kiss.

Jean-Philippe knows very well why Rahim is asking this, but he prefers to put it aside until later. He can only make an important decision with more information.

"The sun's coming up, and I won't be able to go back to sleep. I'll go for a run. It'll clear my head, and I'll be able to think straight. Go back to sleep if you can."

"I'll gladly take an hour's sleep. I've still got the little soldier at attention!"

"I thought I felt a big lump! Tell him he can join me in the shower when I get back, if he's still ready to go to the front line!"

Jean-Philippe kisses Rahim again and gets out of bed. Rahim rolls himself in the covers to continue sleeping.

The March sun has barely risen, casting its light upon the skyscrapers' summits. It ascends leisurely, slowly warming up the English capital. Jean-Philippe closes the door behind him, inhaling the cool air. His warm-up routine commences with stretching everything he can stretch and turning whatever he can turn.

He zips up his jacket before stepping out onto the sidewalk, which has been dampened by the night's rain. Every morning, weather permitting, he jogs through the neighborhood streets. Thanks to his morning run, his energy and his concentration adjust themselves, giving him time to plan his day thoughtfully and effectively. From an early age, Jean-Philippe has struggled with hyperactivity and impulsivity, which have embarrassed him on more than one occasion. Sports, such as cycling and running, were strategies that got him through the long school days. Today, his body craves endorphins for both muscles and spirit. They're a drug he can't give up without going into withdrawal.

Jean-Philippe heads for Victoria Park to get away from the carbon monoxide wafting over London's large boulevards. Merchants pull up the metal curtains of their shops and set up displays in front of their windows, birds chirp gaily, and the fragrance of coffee and bakery goods makes Jean-Philippe salivate. The frenzy of the metropolis is gradually awakening. The hubbub of travel is already forming endless traffic jams. On his new iPhone 3, he selects his sports playlist of upbeat songs. He cranks up the volume as "Viva la Vida", from Coldplay, begins playing. The lyrics, rich in symbolism, resonate in his ears. The song's rhythm elevates his thoughts delving into themes of revolution, conquests, and battling adversities. Jean-Philippe continues to sing the same verses repeatedly. Like the story portrayed in the song, he has fought his way to the top and secured his position at the magazine. He reflects on whether the people in his hometown truly know what he has become.

Indeed, people won't believe what you've become. A journalist for a renowned magazine, but you'll always be a little guy from rural Quebec. You live in a world of unicorns. Any thoughts about your father? He's the one whose face you want

Jean-Philippe frowns as he enters the park. He's never satisfied with himself and constantly accompanied by an inner voice spoiling his fun. He increases his pace.

Delicate pink blossoms appear on the branches of a few precocious cherry trees. Tree buds gently open to make way for the young leaves of oaks and poplars. Victoria Park forms an expanse of green grass, still damp, interspersed with paths used by morning joggers. He greets the usual sportsmen and women before turning toward the cricket fields. He smiles and thinks of Rahim, for whom cricket is like a religion. From his teens to his mid-twenties, Rahim played England's national sport with a passion. Engaging in this team activity helped him manage the anxiety he was experiencing and for which he required assistance.

Jean-Philippe continues in the direction of the English garden to take a break. He catches his breath in front of the old heritage fountain that serves as the center point of his route, one of the many sites being restored in preparation for the Olympic Games scheduled for summer 2012.

In London, as in Montreal before it, Jean-Philippe has jogged his way through the different districts of the metropolis. His feet explored various routes, each district having its own particularities. Conversely, it was his nose and stomach that led him on a quest for pastries, guiding his steps toward the delightful scent and craving for baked goods. His taste buds and sense of smell have complemented his way of discovery. He enjoys croissants, tarts, and cannoli as he strolls along the boulevards. *As long as I burn the calories I consume, there's no shame in it!* he thinks.

You're so afraid of remorse, and yet you eat it by the bucketful! Who are you trying to convince? I'm here, even if you don't listen to me. All it takes is one phone call and I appear...

During his travels, Jean-Philippe frequently utilizes jogging as a means to explore various cities. For instance, while navigating the streets of Sydney, he gained insight into Australia's ethnic minorities, whose contribution have played a significant role in propelling the country to become the economic powerhouse of Oceania. Subsequently, he conducted a report focusing on this subject. What better way to discuss multiculturalism than while stretching one's quadriceps?

While roaming the islands of Stockholm, he engaged with a few Swedes to uncover the secret behind their charm. Jogging fosters many kinds of connections, some less formal than others, but equally delightful. There are diverse ways to explore the world and stretch your gluteal muscles.

Leaving the park, he turns to run along the canal at the rear of the graffiti-strewn warehouses back to his apartment.

2.

A SPOILSPORT'S DAY

March 2010

Jean-Philippe has arranged to meet his colleague Amy at the hotel pub. He enters the room next to the reception, orders a drink from the bar, and chooses a wide, brown leather armchair by the fireplace. This year, Northern Ireland is experiencing a rather cool early spring, so the warmth of the fire mitigates the season's humidity. The flickering of the flames softens the lighting, plunging the clientele into forgetting the usual daily distractions, a moment of recollection much needed by Jean-Philippe. Old, framed newspaper articles decorate the stone walls, and a few antiques adorn the mantelpiece. According to their website, the Bushmills Inn offers spacious, clean rooms in a warm and welcoming environment, in the traditions of country inns. Jean-Philippe has to concede that they live up to his expectations.

The bartender places on the table a glass of water and a Bushmills 10-year-old single malt, an Irish whiskey made in the village's ancestral distillery. After thanking him, Jean-Philippe sets his notepad on the armchair beside him. Although he prefers scotch, he never misses the opportunity to sample the local flavors. Since the beginning of their collaboration, he and Amy have indulged in a tradition of brightening their taste buds during their travels. It's a great way to combine business with pleasure.

Jean-Philippe inhales the whiskey's aroma, detecting notes of vanilla and berries against a woody background. He wets his finger in the glass of water and drops a small amount into the spirit to optimize and accentuate the taste. This technique, shared by Scottish friends, applies superbly to scotch, but is equally suited to Irish or American whiskies. Like a precious possession, he brings the glass to his lips and lets the brandy fill his mouth. The flavor is particularly sweet and more pleasant than he anticipated.

He puts down his glass and opens his notepad to read the information he has gathered since the morning. His notebook never leaves his side. It's his principal working tool, containing factual information as well as thoughts and impressions. Once it's filled in, it ends up in a box with the previous ones in London. Jean-Philippe refers to it whenever he needs inspiration. He writes down all his ideas, no matter how far-fetched. He keeps his old journals, evidence of hard work, and every time he opens the box—which happens frequently—he resolves to organize them by sorting through each by month and year, aiming for more efficient retrieval. However, sitting on the floor, flipping through the books and immersing himself in the nostalgia of past travels makes the exercise considerably more enjoyable. The resolution remains unfinished.

After landing in Belfast, Jean-Philippe met with Professor Albermale, at the suggestion of Mr. Forster, the magazine's associate editor. This eminent researcher specializes in geocriminalistics, also referred to as geographic profiling, which Jean-Philippe is exploring for an article to be published in an upcoming edition of the *World Compass*. He aims to demonstrate how geographical techniques, such as satellite remote sensing or soil analysis, can be employed to solving crimes. Professor Albermale has developed an expertise in the spatial profiling of criminals, helping detectives reduce investigation areas with, at the core of the study, the concept of "distance from the crime."

Jean-Philippe has always had an interest in geography. In fact, his initial enrollment at the university was in this field before he redirected his focus to his other passion, writing. The idea of navigating between those two disciplines gained momentum, which made his integration into the *World Compass* a natural fit.

He thinks about taking the project a step further. He underlines his ideas for a novel with two broad strokes: distance from the crime... Like Kathy Reichs. Anthropology vs. geography?

Pff! You can dream, but you'll never write your novel... You've got ideas. Motivation, not so much.

Amy approaches loudly, disrupting the pub's peaceful atmosphere, and settles down, placing her bottle of Yardsman beer next to Jean-Philippe's Irish whiskey. She sighs heavily before sinking into the lounge chair facing her colleague.

"You're lucky you're not a woman!" she declares. "So much preparation to go out in public."

"I knew you were flirtatious, but not to that extent."

Jean-Philippe stares at her with a mischievous smile, waiting for her to reply. She looks at him, faking insult, and gives him the finger.

"I've combed my hair, I've put on nice clothes, and I smell good! You never know. I might come face to face with Hugh Grant." She laughs. "We're here to celebrate, aren't we?"

She put on a tweed jacket with large buttons over a floral sweater. She's playing the card of sophistication and effortless charm. Her style contrasts with Jean-Philippe's, who is wearing his traditional plaid shirt and cargo pants.

Amy raises her head. She reconnoiters customers, looking for interesting men, ideally single. She lifts her bottle to her lips, followed by a loud burp.

"So much for coquetry!" teases Jean-Philippe.

"Just because I don't drink fancy drinks like yours doesn't mean I can't be coquettish," she objects, raising her hand to stop the discussion. "I like to make myself beautiful for men, but they have to take me as I am."

Despite her yearning for independence, Amy longs to meet her Don Juan, the man of her dreams, the one who will make her heart flutter and her clitoris quiver. A few years ago, she had an intense love affair that ended in turmoil. After the break-up, she became bitter, angry, and melancholic. She decided to invest her energy in her friendship with Jean-Philippe, whom she knew to be loyal.

"I'm only thirty-six, with all its pros and cons."

"Experience comes with soft skin."

"Wait till you get older, and you'll see that your abs of steel will disappear under a layer of fat."

"When I'm fifty, I'll still be working out. I'm going to be a muscle daddy with a beautiful graying beard and pecs to make young people blush." Jean-Philippe laughs. "You know, when I put my mind to something, it's hard to get me to change it."

"A thick-headed guy! I thought you were more attracted to mature men, like Rahim—"

"It's true that he's a bit of an old fart..."

"Old fart! He's my age!"

"You're both pretty old farts!"

The two friends laugh heartily, an outlet for the negative energy struggling to drain away. Jean-Philippe's thoughts wander between the happiness of being in Northern Ireland with his best friend and worries about his family.

"I'm convinced that as you get older, you have to make choices when it comes to love: it's either passion or the circus, but hey, I'm done with the pirouettes! I don't have the flexibility I had as a teenager." She laughs again. "As for passion, let's just say that men don't complain about it."

"That's how I love you, my friend. Without barriers and fully assumed. But please, no details."

"I could teach you a thing or two you could do with your handsome Rahim!" suggests Amy.

"I'm quite happy with what I have," he reassures her. "I'm still able to play in the 'pirouette' phase."

"Stop bragging. You know I'm sex-starved. The next guy better be in shape!"

Jean-Philippe raises his glass and Amy her bottle to toast their friendship.

"I love you, old girl! I wouldn't trade you for the world."

Four years earlier, Jean-Philippe and Amy undertook their first coverage together in Malaysia, focusing on the sacred sites of Kuala Lumpur. Between a laksa dish and satay skewers, Jean-Philippe felt an instant connection with Amy, quickly forming a strong friendship. Behind her caustic facade, he discovered a generous heart. They spent every week together. Like two teenagers in a shopping mall, they gossiped about anything and everything, especially men's butts. A consensus formed that a bulging ass in tight pants was their favorite.

Amy amused herself with street children by taking their picture or imitating a monkey. In the Batu caves, playing ventriloquist, she joked with the macaques and roosters that invaded the temple: "Get a grip, fatso," "You come here often?" and "I'm free at 4:00, wanna get a room?"

With too much laughter, Jean-Philippe had to step aside out of respect for the Hindu shrine. Today, their complicity surpasses the bonds of work.

"Here's to new challenges!" exclaims Amy, unconcerned about disturbing the pub's patrons.

"I can't believe I'm going to have my own column. Do you realize they accepted my project on the spot?" Jean-Philippe blushes at the thought.

"Why wouldn't they? Did you doubt it?"

"Let's just say—"

"Well, it's true!" she cuts in. "You're always doubting yourself!"

"Doubt is a writer's lifeblood. We're doing a trial run with five columns, and we'll reassess afterward."

"You're an excellent journalist, JeanPea. I'm delighted every time I read your articles. You have such a sensitive way of telling the stories of our travels. I feel privileged to be part of the team," says Amy.

"Stop that!"

"No, you stop the false modesty. JeanPea, tonight, we're celebrating you, and I'm ordering a new round!"

Unable to pronounce his first name, Amy calls him JeanPea, like the pants and the green vegetable, his French name being too long anyway, according to her. Jean-Philippe Genest became JeanPea Jenny, a name that crystallized among his colleagues at the magazine. On the contrary, Jean-Philippe rolls his Rs when he speaks English, revealing his French accent. Amy laughs when he says her last name, Cromarty, with two Rs.

Traveling on every continent for the past five years, Jean-Philippe has written numerous articles for the *World Compass*. Distributed worldwide, the magazine features articles on geography, travel, people, and culture. For the new column, he has been given the freedom to put together his own team and has obviously enlisted Amy's help, which came as no surprise to anyone at the magazine. The column, entitled "The Mythographers," will start this summer. Jean-Philippe promises to revisit ancient myths through the scientific lens of the 21st century.

For him, it's a dream come true, a wonderful way to tell stories—mixing earth sciences with goddesses, monsters, and magic, providing scientific explanations while writing about ogres and witches. Jean-Philippe got the idea while visiting Mount Etna in Sicily, the home of the Greek god Hephaestus. The Roman god Vulcan became associated with what are now referred to as volcanoes, and it's from him that the name for these geological formations is derived.

Jean-Philippe dips into his notebook and Amy notices his preoccupied expression.

"Still no news from your mother?"

"Nothing. My father has to take some tests. I imagine it'll take a while to get the results."

Jean-Philippe takes off his glasses and puts his hair back in place, tying it with a rubber band at the back of his head.

"Look at you, talking about me. If there's anyone stylish between us, it's you. Your hair is longer than mine!" Amy teases him.

"It's a question of efficiency. When you don't have time to comb it, you just tie it up and that's it," he sums up as he puts his glasses back on.

The bartender brings refills of their drinks.

"We have to get up early tomorrow. I don't know if I should..." he says, pointing at the glasses.

"You're only thirty, and you're softer than I am! We've only got one life to live! YOLO!" she shouts.

Jean-Philippe smiles and grabs his glass, banging it against Amy's. He's always overdoing it. He worries too much. He broods over everything in his mind, a perpetual whirlwind that hinders access to his innermost thoughts. Only Amy has the ability to break through the barrier of his mind and make him react.

"I'm still hesitating about my angle for the column. Where should I begin: the science or the myth?"

"What does your gut tell you?" asks Amy.

"Logically, it would be to approach the text through myth. After all, the editors accepted my proposal on the basis of the legends."

"You see, you've got the answers. JeanPea, stop doubting yourself!"

Where would you be without doubts? You breathe doubts, you taste doubts, you make your bed under a quilt of doubts. And I like reminding you of that.

More than anything else, Jean-Philippe wants to make people's culture accessible through their legends by giving them new lives in print. He has convinced publishers to promote little-known traditions and compare them with current scientific knowledge, without sacrificing folklore in order to bring it to life.

He imposes on himself the pressure to excel in order to honor the editors' trust. From a very young age, he has made it his mandate to perform well, at school, in sports, and in his relationships. It's a burden that weighs heavily on his shoulders.

Knowing Northern Ireland well, having visited it with his mentor when he was a trainee in the early days, he puts every chance on his side. For the first installment, he has chosen the Giant's Causeway in County Antrim. The spectacularly beautiful site serves the legend well.

"Tomorrow morning, I want to be on site at sunrise. I think the colors during the golden hour will be magnificent. It'll be a sight to behold for the first column," says Amy reassuringly.

"What I'd like to do is orient the photo to show the extension of the Giant's Causeway into the sea," suggests Jean-Philippe.

"I've written it all down. I'm going to play with the exposure and give the water a wispy effect. I think you'll like it."

"Close-ups of the cobblestones, the walls, the columns, and… I forgot, we'll be climbing onto the promontory, onto the roof of the visitor center, to get wide shots of the Antrim plateau."

"Brilliant idea! The perspective will be excellent from above. We'll be able to capture the cliffs, the causeway, and the sea. Don't forget to put on a hat and a good coat; it's likely to be chilly."

"Yes, Mommy!"

Jean-Philippe isn't worried about the quality of the photos. Amy is the most qualified and talented photographer he knows. He simply wants to play his role as artistic director for the first feature.

His iPhone rings. He retrieves his device from the chair and sees that a voice message is being recorded.

"I'll take a message and come back. I don't understand why I didn't hear it," he apologizes.

He steps out into the hall to listen to the message:

"Hi Phil, it's Mom! I wanted to give you an update. Your father hasn't finished with his tests. He's had blood tests and X-rays. It wasn't clear, but the doctor saw spots. She didn't know if they're benign or malignant. She didn't like what she saw, and I don't like it either. Of course, with his backache and his sprained ankle, he won't be able to walk for a while, but there's no concussion. I'm calling from the hospital, so it might be hard to talk again today, and I don't even know what time it is where you are. Anyway, call me later when I get home. Okay, I'm hanging up. Bye!"

Jean-Philippe returns slowly to his chair, looking serious.

"Any news?" Amy asks.

"Yes. It's a bit confusing. When my mother gets upset, she talks fast and forgets bits and pieces. My father is not in great shape. What I understand is that his doctor wants to do more analysis. Mom mentioned spots on the X-rays, and that my father will have to undergo further tests. Sounds pretty complex."

"Are you going to see him?"

"I don't know. I'm not sure. I'm hesitating."

"When was your last visit to Quebec?"

"Five years ago."

"And you don't miss it?"

"I sure do. I'd love to hug my mother. I don't know about my father. Let's just say that we don't have the best of relationships. But I spent my childhood very close to him. Every day, we spent some time together and every night, he read me bedtime stories. We were the best of friends."

"My father didn't do that for me!"

"But at some point, I'm not sure when, we lost touch. He didn't understand me, or he just didn't want to. That was when he became mayor of our village. He wanted a model family, and I wasn't the wisest boy. I was so different from my brother Felix. I think he would have wanted me to be like him."

"You surprise me!" Amy says with a laugh.

"I demanded everything. The teenage years weren't easy. I knew I was different, without really knowing how to explain it at the time. I knew I didn't want to stay there. The countryside wasn't for me. I moved away to attend college and university. I made my life in Montreal. I was free, and when I came back to Ithaca-on-the-Lake, I felt like I was going back in time. At some point, things fell apart, and we haven't spoken since."

"Don't you want to go back to him? Reconnect?"

"Him and me? It's a long shot! Two stubborn guys, and proud ones at that. It won't be easy!"

In 2005, a rift developed between Jean-Philippe and his father, each sitting on their positions like two islands drifting in the ocean. His mother Michelle carries the conflict between her husband and son on her shoulders and holds onto hope that the fractured relationship between the two men can be repaired. Neither has taken the first steps toward reconciliation and, as the years go by, the rift only widens.

Alone on his continent, Jean-Philippe was rescued by Amy—or vice versa. With her, he has built a solid refuge, a deep-rooted protection, which he isn't ready to leave. Today, he understands that his island continues to drift, and he's one saboteur away from sinking. His greatest enemy remains himself.

3.

FOG-BRAINED

March 2010

As he enters his apartment, Jean-Philippe looks at the clock and hurries up. His suitcase isn't packed, and Rahim is on his way. In the middle of the hall, he kicks off his shoes, places his iPhone and his watch on the living room table, and tosses his sweaty clothes onto the sofa. He runs naked to the bathroom to turn on the shower. As he heads back to his desk nestled in the corner of the living room, he opens his laptop to review and print his travel documents.

Jean-Philippe loves his apartment. On two levels, his bedroom and that of Luke, his roommate, are on the top floor. He earns a respectable salary at the *World Compass*, not quite enough to pay for accommodation of this type in London, but Luke's share gives him financial space to breathe. Spacious and well-lit thanks to the large windows, the rent will inevitably rise when gentrification reaches Hackney. London is already one of the world's most expensive metropolises, and Jean-Philippe can't imagine the years after the 2012 Olympic Games. In the meantime, he's enjoying the apartment alone, as Luke is on tour with his theater company for a few weeks. Jean-Philippe looks at the housework to be done and tells himself that cleaning will have to wait—again. Various jumbled documents cover the small table that serves as his office. His plate and glass from this morning lay on the end of the counter, and the plants are wilting.

He steps into the shower and slides his head under the water stream. The hot water numbs his face, but his heart pounds in his chest to the point that his ribcage is heaving. With his hands on the ceramic wall, he forces himself to take deep breaths to avoid further dizziness. He manages to slow down the spiral of panic that has controlled his brain for the last week. He meditates and imagines himself in his "happy place," which takes the shape of his teenage bedroom. When jogging and lifting weights at the gym fail to relax him, it's because stress has overwhelmed his mind. He needs to refocus.

The fog gradually clears up. In his mind, wherever his eyes land, Jean-Philippe relives his childhood memories. Next to his bed, columns of books are stacked with novels and comic books. His bicycle rests below the basement window. His red-and-black helmet hangs by the strap from the curved handlebars. In a corner, all his running shoes with worn-out soles remind him of all the kilometers he's run. When he left Ithaca-on-the-Lake to live in Montreal, he switched from cycling to jogging, a more practical sport in an urban environment.

His clothes are piled up on the dresser, on the floor, or overflowing from the drawers, but never in the laundry basket. His heart slowly calms in this comforting chaos. His grocery store polo shirt, the one he wore when he got his first job as a student, and his cycling vest lie on the back of the office chair. He glimpses the photos of muscular men, usually shirtless, in their underwear or Speedos, protruding from their hiding place between the mattress and the box spring. He smiles as he discovers the box of tissues just below. Next to the bedside lamp, he stares at the portrait of Rahim with his beautiful, silky black hair, just as it was when they first met. The walls are decorated with a large map of the world and posters of *Indiana Jones* and *Back to the Future*. He can almost hear the movies' soundtracks. His room is his memory lair, his scrapbook. At a glance, he can see his life—that is, the life he wanted to project.

Jean-Philippe's body begins to float imperceptibly above the carpet, with a strange force dragging him slowly toward the huge wooden door in the corner of the room. Despite the strong sun glaring down, the light refuses to submit in this corner of the room. He levitates, inching closer to the door, which disappears, making way for an enormous chest lit by a small light bulb. Jean-Philippe knows the contents of this box, having filled it himself with all the memories he wanted to bury and hide. The trunk creaks each time it's opened, and the latch sticks. The ropes and ribbons can no longer hold the padlocked lid in place. He tried so hard to barricade the crate; now it's bursting open, bombarding his face and torso with remnants, reminders, and traces of the past. Thousands of snapshots fly out and slam into his cheeks. The photos flood the floor and Jean-Philippe falls on his back, buried by his memory, which awakens in a strange way.

"Big doofus!"
"Why aren't you like your brother?"
"It's Jean-Philippe's fault!"
"You'll never see my face again!"
Nice memories, don't you think?

The room spins round and round. He hears his heartbeats like a tambourine. Gasping and staggering, Jean-Philippe turns off the water and steps out of the shower. His legs wobble, so he grabs the towel rod. He can't believe what's happening. All it took was a call from his mother to bring back his past. For the past five years, he has been making a new life for himself in London. Amy and Rahim know only a few fragments of it, the ones he has been willing to share.

The box is his baggage, an emotional burden. In his eagerness to start afresh, he has buried all his past, the positive as well as the negative. The last few discussions with his father were so conflictual that any association of his name or face causes him great gloom. Jean-Philippe has barricaded his past in a crate. He even enclosed his "happy place," his bedroom, behind a wall. He has locked himself in and prevented others from entering, for fear of opening the door to a time long past.

It's no longer a question of returning memories to their trunk, but of confronting them. Time doesn't resolve conflicts, and neither does fleeing. It's time to clean up. He only has two choices: assume or destroy.

Ironically, the first trace that emerges coincides with his dad's last insult: "Big doofus!" The movie of his past reminds him of every moment when his father uttered these words, words that hurt. Jean-Philippe takes his courage in both hands and pins this memory to the wall of his mind.

In the small bathroom, steam floats in the air. With a sweep of his arm, he wipes the condensation from the mirror but blurs visibility with the large streaks through the glass. Using the hair dryer, he blows out a section wide enough to see his reflection. He puts on his glasses, which give him a nerdy look. He's chosen round, black frames, the same ones worn by Robert Downey Jr. in an interview for the film *Iron Man*. He thinks he looks cool. Between deep breaths, he stares at his beard and decides that he won't be shaving. That's the advantage of blond hair: a three-day beard lasts a week. He untangles his long hair out of habit and dries it at maximum power to save time. Finally, he ties it up in a bun behind his head.

Jean-Philippe pulls the thin skin of his stomach in front of his abs and compliments himself on keeping them visible, despite his hectic schedule. He enjoys working out and appreciates the image he projects. He knows the quest for the perfect body is superficial, but futility became an obsession; now it's a necessity. He likes to turn heads. It's pretentious, but he assumes it. He knows that as he gets older, it'll be harder to keep in shape, but in the meantime, he doesn't have to deprive himself of pastries.

He removes the towel from around his neck and inspects his pecs. His phoenix tattoo sits enthroned on his bicep, its wings covering the entire left pectoral muscle. He admires this mythical animal rising from the ashes. Jean-Philippe began a new life in London and created a new existence, but now he sees it didn't work.

Raising his arm, he feels a slight pain in his shoulder that bothers him. Since his return from Belfast, Jean-Philippe has given his all, both in running and in the gym. Five kilometers every morning and two hours pushing iron, but nothing is helping. The weight of memories outweighs the dumbbells. This week's conversations with his mother upset him, and despite all the energy he expended, insomnia set in. He tossed and turned all night. To help himself fall asleep, he read, walked around the apartment, drank a large glass of water, turned on the TV, then turned it back off after a few minutes of channel surfing. He barely slept three hours, which is clearly not enough. Pockets have appeared under his reddened eyes.

He looks in the mirror and sees a gloomy version of himself, devoid of the joyful essence he once had. Fatigue affects his morale. He becomes more impulsive, and negative thoughts take over. Whether it's procrastination or simply running away, his inner saboteur is sending him messages he can't listen to right now. He pulls himself together and picks up the pace to complete his preparations.

All week, he deliberated about returning to Quebec. It was finally his mother's call last night that precipitated his decision. Later that day, his father will be undergoing a risky operation and, whether he likes it or not, he has decided to go to his bedside. Despite his resentment, Jean-Philippe has booked a last-minute plane ticket for the 12:30 flight to Montreal. His decision is made: he will return to Ithaca-on-the-Lake to confront his past, if the gods allow him to arrive in time.

Are you ready to go home? Are you ready to see your father again? You're afraid, admit it!

At the center of his mind, in his teenage bedroom, sitting amid his memories, every image he holds in his hand reminds him of his father. Over the past week, Jean-Philippe has realized that he must put aside his pride and stop waiting for excuses from his father. Time is of the essence.

Damn stubborn minded! Did you really think he was going to apologize?

With time and distance, he has taken a step back. After five years, Jean-Philippe naively believed that the bitterness of the last conversations at his parents' house would have disappeared. His mind still wavers between guilt and resentment, all mixed with great sadness. On the one hand, he's depriving himself of a family, and on the other, he's living with animosity toward his father, his fallen hero. This fixation with separating his past from his present has kept the wound open. Jean-Philippe believed that by moving abroad, he would be able to start afresh, with a new job and new friends. But it's clear that he can't recreate his family. Rahim is there, but Jean-Philippe keeps him away from his past. His mother doesn't even know he's had a boyfriend for two years. There's only one solution: to have a real discussion with his father, a step essential for his true liberation.

"JP?" calls Rahim.

"I'm in the bathroom," shouts Jean-Philippe through the door.

He splashes his face with cold water to erase the weight of memories and puts on an uncertain smile. He ties the large, white towel around his waist and takes a long breath before stepping outside the bathroom. He tosses the small hand towel to the laundry basket; it lands on the floor next to it. Rahim is collecting the items of clothing scattered around the living room and over the kitchen chairs. He finally picks up the hand towel and buries it in the basket. He has even lined up the shoes along the wall.

His boyfriend plumps up the cushions and arranges them on his gray sofa while Jean-Philippe admires him. Rahim smiles with pride at the satisfactory arrangement. He stands with his back straight and his fists on his hips, still wearing his Charles Tyrwhitt jacket, Paul Smith shirt, and Oxford shoes. Rahim, the man of tradition and habit, the archetypal British gentleman in both personality and posture, reassures Jean-Philippe, the worried, the chaotic, the unpredictable.

He approaches Rahim and kisses him gently. He runs his hand over his cheek, because he loves to touch his soft, freshly shaved skin, savoring the delightful fragrance it carries. Rahim moisturizes with high-quality balms and essential oils. Jean-Philippe recognizes the scent of bergamot and vanilla. He remembers one morning, after a suave night, he opened a jar of cream to inhale Rahim's scent. His lover came in behind and hugged him, kissing his sensitive neck. He turned around and sat on the marble counter of the huge bathroom. Rahim moistened his finger with cream and rubbed it gently over his forehead, under his eyes, on his cheeks and nose. Jean-Philippe offered himself as a canvas and, after applying scented cream to each part of his face, Rahim kissed him. Jean-Philippe smiled, knowing he would be carrying his lover's scent around with him for the rest of the day.

He holds him close, like a child afraid of losing his toy. Rahim takes advantage of their closeness to run his hand down his lover's hip in the hope of removing the towel, but Jean-Philippe holds back his hand despite his mad desire to make love. His preparations aren't complete; his mind is preoccupied, his body fatigued. Despite the desire, his sexual organ doesn't respond. With a little more time, he would have continued to kiss his lover, because Rahim has the most tender lips in the world.

"I've got a-a flight at 12:30," he stammers as he heads for the staircase to the bedrooms.

"What do you mean, a flight? You were in Belfast last week. You told me your next report was at the end of the month!" Rahim worries aloud, surprised by this change in schedule. "Yemen, I think."

Rahim checks his phone to make sure he has the right information. He knows all Jean-Philippe's plans. He keeps his diary, his main working tool, close at hand, like Jean-Philippe does with his notebook. He always provides him with his flight schedules and Rahim compiles everything, an effective way of controlling his anxiety. Since he has many meetings to attend, his calendar allows him to live out his week serenely. It's a strategy that works well for him.

"I thought we were spending the weekend here?" asks Rahim. "I even had tickets for *Legally Blonde, The Musical* at the Savoy Theater. You've been telling me about it for ages."

"Shit! I forgot all about it. Are you going to be able to exchange them?"

"I'll have to; I'm not going there alone!"

Jean-Philippe and Rahim usually spend their weekends together, in Jean-Philippe's apartment in the borough of Hackney or in Canary Wharf. Rahim owns a condo on the 17th floor of a luxury complex in the business district on Harbord Square. Rahim has invited him to come and live with him, but Jean-Philippe has always refused. He claims he wants to maintain his independence.

Bullshit!

They avoid talking about it, a bone of contention between the two. Jean-Philippe doesn't want to raise rumors that their relationship is based on money.

Bullshit!

As Rahim is considerably wealthier than Jean-Philippe, he uses their economic status as an excuse. Jean-Philippe knows this is bullshit. He also knows it's fear. Fear of not measuring up. Fear of being vulnerable. To create a future, you have to merge the past, and Jean-Philippe isn't ready to include Rahim in his story, a story he has tried to erase until now.

"You don't have to work overtime. You know that if there's a problem, I can take care of it," offers Rahim.

"No, it's not that. I'm leaving for Montreal," replies Jean-Philippe curtly.

He pulls the suitcase from under the bed and begins to fill it with clothes. He moves between the dresser and the bed, not really thinking about what he's putting in or in what order: socks, boxers, t-shirts, sweaters, jeans, pants, shirts.

"It's my dad, he's in the hospital," Jean-Philippe defends himself nervously.

"That doesn't mean anything. Your mother will give you news like she always does! You mustn't worry too much," he reassures him, but adds, "Not long ago, you said it was stressing you out to think about going back home. You avoid contracts that come close to Canada. We can take a moment to discuss it. You know I'm open, and I'd like to know more about you and your family."

"You'll never see my face again!" Not keeping your promises now?

"You don't get it. My father's having surgery today. I've got to go. My mother talked about cancer, and we don't know how serious it is."

"An operation? For cancer? You just found out? It's not the same thing as falling off a ladder."

Rahim, the pragmatist, the one who analyzes every situation, is telling the truth, but Jean-Philippe's emotions are overpowering whatever rational capacities he has left. He would like to slow down to think, to plan, because he can't land in Ithaca-on-the-Lake after five years as if nothing has happened. But he doesn't have the luxury of time. His father could die before he has had a chance to explain and apologize. Faced with the fear of remorse, Jean-Philippe finds himself backed into a corner.

"My mother called me at the beginning of the week."

"We talk every day and you're only telling me today? You told me about your new column. You told me about Amy, and you didn't tell me about your father. I'm a little confused. Crap! I'm your partner. I have no desire to relive stories of secrecy. It always ends badly; I know what I'm talking about. I thought you had enough self-esteem to confide in me."

There's a long silence in the room. Jean-Philippe sits on the edge of the bed, removes his glasses, and rubs his eyes. He looks at the floor and lets out a downhearted moan through his clenched jaws, a concentrated distress buried deep in his lungs.

Rahim sighs phlegmatically and slides the suitcase gently toward him. He starts replacing the pieces of clothing in his luggage.

Jean-Philippe stares aimlessly out the window.

"I told myself I had time. I told myself he'd take the first step," he murmurs wistfully. "Every day, every week, every month, it's harder and harder to reconnect with him. We haven't spoken in five years. I'm not the same man anymore, I'm somewhere else. There was a split, and we've been separating ever since. We're drifting apart without looking at each other."

His heart pumps blood to his head like a volcano ready to erupt. The arteries in his neck pulse. His mental pendulum loses its stability. The balance he has maintained all these years is artificial. Yet Jean-Philippe is determined to preserve this tranquility. His past is staring him in the face, and he feels guilty for a fault for which he accepts no responsibility.

You'll be rejected again! That's how he'll react when he sees you. And you won't know how to defend yourself.

He bows his head and only the sound of rustling fabric behind him can be heard.

"You're quite handsome, Babe, but you're still going to have to get dressed. They won't let you on the plane with only your towel on!" Rahim laughs to lighten the mood.

Babe, a sweet little word with deep meaning. Never has a man touched his inner self as Rahim does with this loving nickname. Since he was a teenager, to hide his orientation, to change his image, Jean-Philippe has erected gigantic barriers that only a few people have been able to break through. He knows that the walls still stand, thicker and stronger than ever. Now a master of mental masonry and comfortably ensconced behind those walls, he must return to Ithaca-on-the-Lake to tear them down.

He stands up to kiss Rahim on the neck and hold him close. He opens a drawer to select more travel clothes. He takes advantage of the moment to place his laptop, notepad, and book in his backpack. He will add his iPhone and the watch he left in the living room. He puts away his travel kit while Rahim finishes folding the shirts to prevent them wrinkling.

"If you'd told me, I could have gone with you," says Rahim, himself surprised to have uttered the phrase.

"I made my decision last night. I've had little or no sleep for a week. My mother told me that the doctor is going to operate to remove part of the cancer," he says with a bitter taste as he utters the name of the disease. "Besides, it's not in your nature to be so spontaneous."

For Rahim, a trip like this requires hours of preparation and planning, writing lists of telephone numbers for carriers, hotels, embassies, and so on. Rahim has immense qualities, an exceptional human being, but with an anxious temperament that's part of his charm.

"Yes, you're quite right about that," he says.

"I've got to tell you something too: my parents don't know I've got a boyfriend," Jean-Philippe quietly slips in.

Rahim looks at him with an expression somewhere between surprise and sadness. He hesitates before replying to make sure he's heard correctly.

"We've been seeing each other for almost two years, and they don't know I exist?" he asks. "You're telling me that your mother calls in the middle of the night and she has no idea that I'm lying next to you!"

"I've never been able to tell her. Whenever I've talked about my orientation with her, it's always created discomfort."

"It's been several years now. At some point, you have to be brave and move on."

"We'll talk about courage when you're ready to face up to your own fears," he says, knowing that his words have gone beyond his thoughts.

"Be careful what you say. It's not the same context at all." Rahim frowns, straightening up and staring at Jean-Philippe.

"I don't need to relive disappointments. My life's been full of them lately," he replies, overwhelmed.

"It's not that difficult."

"We're not all perfect like you." Jean-Philippe instantly regrets the words that come out of his mouth, but he doesn't have time to deal with his relationship with Rahim. "Right now, what I need to know is if you'll drive me to the airport or if I call a cab?"

To: <u>amy.cromarty@worldcompass.com</u>

Hi Amy,

I'm sending you the first draft of our first Mythographer: "The Giant's Causeway." Let me know what you think. Can you look for photos we could put in it? I know I'm asking a lot of you, but I think you can sort through your images, and we can come up with a more complete version before sending it to Mr. Forster.

I was reading it again and I had no idea that a legend like that could speak to me so much. I love the myth and the site is beautiful. But the story appeals to me. You know, this story about creating a bridge between the two giants is like forcing myself to create one between my father and me. Both of us, on our respective continents. That's when you realize that not all bridges are made of concrete!

See you soon, my friend,

J.P.

The Mythographers

A BRIDGE FOR GIANTS

By Jean-Philippe Genest
Photographs by Amy Cromarty

When a country has a legendary hero named Finn MacCool, destiny is good. Admit it: it's a name well-suited for a Hollywood movie character. In Celtic mythology, Finn MacCool is an Irish giant with golden hair from the Fianna clan, mainly composed of warriors and mercenaries traveling the roads of Ireland.

Its reputation extends beyond the country's borders. He defeated the fairy Aillen, who put men to sleep before reducing their palace to ashes. He created the Isle of Man by throwing part of Irish territory into the sea. A bit impulsive, you might say. This clearly demonstrates the fiery character of the Irish.

On the other side of the strait lives another giant, a Scottish one, named Benandonner. Known for his strength and outspokenness, his rival insults Finn MacCool without scruples. He mocks his exploits, even though they are endorsed by the entire Gaelic nation.

Finn must settle the discord once and for all and preserve his Celtic pride. He begins the construction of a bridge between Ulster and Scotland by dismantling columns of basalt, which he throws into the sea. Relentlessly, he breaks down the cliffs to build the road which will take him toward his adversary in order to clear up their differences strewn with insults and arrogance. Impulsive but delicate, there was no question of swimming or getting wet. The giants don't like to put their feet in the water, hence the need to build this route!

At the end of the crossing, Finn finally perceives the gigantic stature of his competitor, a dimension clearly underestimated on his part. Panicked, MacCool runs home. A few moments later, the villagers hear the deafening strides of the Scot shaking the houses all along the coast. Finn then asks his wife Oonagh for advice.

Quickly, Oonagh disguises her husband as an infant whom she lays in the bathtub. When Benandonner arrives at the MacCool home, she presents him with her young child pretending to be waiting for her husband. The Scottish giant runs wild, unable to imagine defeating a colossus that would have produced a baby of this size. He turns around, destroying the roadway in the process.

The myth offers variations depending on the authors. Some write that Oonagh offers Benandonner a stone, presenting it as a piece of bread, but he loses his teeth when he bites into the food. When she gives the bread—real bread—to her child, the Scottish giant can only see the strength of Finn MacCool's son and runs away.

The road is never used again and disappears under the ocean. Ultimately, perhaps it is Oonagh who should be celebrated. She was the one who resolved the impasse.

From myth to geology

North of Bushmills, a stone path built centuries ago can be seen on the north Ulster coast. For the Irish, these "ruins" known as the Giant's Causeway correspond to the starting point of a road which leads to Scotland. Seen from the sky, the site allows one to imagine a path paved and laid out with small hexagonal stones, like in medieval streets. The very wide causeway plunges into the sea toward Scotland.

The Giant's Causeway, a major tourist attraction and a UNESCO World Heritage site since 1986, brings together both volcanology admirers and legend enthusiasts. The Antrim plateau, which makes up most of Northern Ireland, was formed by successive flows of basalt lava dating back sixty million years. By rapidly cooling, the lava contracted and fractured, giving this cobblestone appearance on the surface. Over time, erosion has sculpted masterful works worthy of a titan's apartment. Here, an organ whose basalt columns recall the pipes of a large cathedral organ. There, a staircase and a series of pistons moving up and down. For a brief moment, it is possible to hear, in the blowing of the wind, the notes of a Celtic score.

The consecration of the legend of the Giant's Causeway is enriched by the existence, on the island of Staffa in Scotland, of a collection of basalt pillars similar to those of the Antrim plateau. Located on the other side of the sea, the island would coincide with the other end of the Giant's Causeway.

The myth of Finn MacCool is at the heart of Irish folklore, both north and south. Thanks to national pride carried through song, dance, and literature, Irish culture shines with boldness internationally. The camaraderie and hospitality of the locals is expressed through stories, food, and beer. So, sit in a pub and listen to the lively conversations. Pay a round and become lifelong friends with Finn MacCool, but don't insult him or you might end up breaking your teeth on a sandwich served between two stones!

Between legend and science, it is now up to you, dear readers, to decide the origin of the Giant's Causeway.

A bridge worthy of Finn MacCool?

The idea of a bridge linking Northern Ireland and Scotland has been part of politicians' plans for several decades. But how to connect two coasts that are forty-five kilometers apart? From election to election, projects take shape and disappear as quickly as a pint of Guinness in front of an Irishman. The astronomical costs, running into billions of pounds, and engineering challenges raise the question of the feasibility of uniting these two regions. For human beings, the need to build bridges is essential. Whether it is concrete or emotional, humans are beings of relationships and contacts. How far will they go to bring people together? Will the construction of the bridge remain a dream?

Relationships are at the heart of communities. Certain contacts bring us together and certain fault lines separate us. A word of advice: don't let the faults widen because, over time, longer bridges will have to be built.

Welcome to The Mythographers!

The World Compass, July 2010

4.

A NOSTALGIC STORM

March 2010

Spring in Montreal is similar to winter in London, when rain and sleet mix with snow. The cool wind blows Jean-Philippe's coat, which he hastens to fasten closed while dragging his suitcase to the taxi zone.

"Can you take me… Oops, sorry. I have to go to St. Menelaus Hospital," he corrects himself in French.

The driver stows the suitcase in the trunk of the vehicle and accelerates swiftly. Jean-Philippe presses his nose to the window and contemplates the changes in the Montreal landscape made up of highways and skyscrapers. The cab crosses a bridge to the north, and he finally sees some greenery. The radio reports that the traffic is quite fluid this afternoon. Following that, "Don't Speak" by the group No Doubt fills the cab, evoking memories of Jean-Philippe's early twenties, ten years ago. Despite the song talking about a break-up, the nostalgia within this power ballad reminds him of the loss of someone special, like a family member.

Summer 2000

The female singer has a badass appearance, the one he wishes he could adopt for himself. During that entire summer, he has attended concerts with the sole intention of fantasizing about kissing either the guitarist or the drummer. Jean-Philippe goes out to the Montreal Gay Village several times a week. He walks on Sainte Catherine Street and frequents popular bars and nightclubs. He is finally enjoying his freedom and the spirit of community, he who felt alone in Ithaca-on-the-Lake.

He drinks a lot of beer. A lot. He dances at Club Sky to the music of Daft Punk, very popular this year. He sings on karaoke nights and attends drag queen performances at Mado's Cabaret. Jean-Philippe takes full advantage of the weekend that offers different programming, like a child in front of a plate of candy, hoping to taste everything. Between classes at university, his job as a waiter in a restaurant, and his activities, the nights are short. At least he has Mondays off, which allows him to rest.

With his friends Jake and Mathieu, he parties until late at night. Obviously, he fucks other guys. Often. Really often. Without much subtlety, the men approach him on the dance floor, rubbing their hips on his round buttocks, which he proudly displays. With his blond hair and his svelte look, he categorizes himself as a twink and attracts attention and desire.

Sometimes he acts indifferent to increase his sex appeal even if, inside, he thrives on the attention. In the game of seduction, the merry-go-round can turn out to be dangerous. If the seducer loses interest, it's Jean-Philippe's esteem that crumbles.

He regularly meets athletic men with imposing muscles. He loves their virility, the strength and power they display. When chemistry manifests, the sex proves exhilarating, intoxicating, matching Jean-Philippe's teenage fantasies. He meets guys a few times, never more. He also happens to meet a few egocentrics who only use him as a simple receptacle, men whom Jean-Philippe leaves in the middle of the night—a sex shipwreck in the ocean of his desires.

Not pretty enough? Not interesting enough? Just an ass?

March 2010

Jean-Philippe understands what it means to make love with Rahim. For the past two years, he has fallen asleep in the arms of his friend, his lover, his love, holding Rahim's body against his, feeling his warmth and breath on his neck. Jean-Philippe is a great romantic who is unaware of himself.

And you still don't want to have that every night! Big doofus!

The taxi stops at the hospital's main entrance. Patients walk around in gowns, some with their coats on their shoulders, while others drag their IV pole and smoke cigarettes. A nurse speaks on the phone, gesturing, as visitors sneak into the facility. Jean-Philippe pays the driver, who then goes to the trunk and places the suitcase on the sidewalk.

As he opens the cab door, Jean-Philippe's foot lands in the slush, and his shoe absorbs the icy water. He yells a hearty, "Fuck!" Stretching his leg to reach the sidewalk, he hopes that the incident isn't a sign of impending misfortune. With his backpack on, he limps toward the entrance, suitcase by his side, leaning on his heel. Despite his efforts, his toes shiver in his damp sock.

Too late, the taxi left. Too late, your father may be dead! You're going to be stuck with regrets your whole life. Too late, too late!

Jean-Philippe wipes the sweat from his forehead. His breathing quickens, and his brain blasts him with dozens of images per second. He contemplates the building standing out with its impregnable fortress façade and its gray concrete levels. He enters through the revolving doors toward the gallows. One step at a time, he limps to the information desk to confront his past.

Ever since he can remember, Jean-Philippe has always asked a lot of questions. To satisfy his boundless curiosity, his father Marc responds to his thirst for learning every evening before bed. It becomes a ritual. He reads stories to his son, which then serve as topics for their discussions. Yet *Around the World in Eighty Days* by Jules Verne invariably shapes his evenings.

"The distance between Suez and Aden is precisely thirteen hundred and ten miles…" his father recounts.

"Where is Aden?" questions Jean-Philippe.

"Wait, I'll get the atlas to show you."

Marc stands up to retrieve a large, hefty book. Jean-Philippe can't believe his eyes; he's astonished that a book of this size exists.

"It's in South Yemen. At the bottom, just south of the Red Sea. So, they depart from Suez in Egypt, heading across the Red Sea, right there. And thirteen hundred and ten miles, that's a little over two thousand kilometers," replies Marc, tracing the route with his finger on the map of the Middle East. Then he continues, reading from the book. "The regulations of the company allow the steamers one hundred and thirty-eight hours in which to traverse it." Mentally calculating, he adds, "That's a little less than six days."

He recites further from the novel, "The *Mongolia*, thanks to the vigorous exertions of the engineer, seemed likely, so rapid was her speed, to reach her destination considerably within that time."

"Why don't they take the plane?" asks Jean-Philippe.

"Because planes haven't been invented yet. Remember that the story takes place in 1872, and it wasn't until 1903 that the Wright brothers flew the first aircraft, and only for one minute. We're still far from flying passengers as we do today!"

"Have you ever flown on a plane?"

"No, never."

"But you build them!"

"Yes, but someone else pilots them. It's expensive, you know."

"Would you like that?"

"Yes, absolutely," confides Marc. "Maybe if you and your brother behave yourselves, we could plan a trip to Florida. I'm sure your mother would like that."

"Wow! One day, I'll be the one to take you on a trip!" he promises proudly.

"For now, time to go to bed. We'll continue this chapter tomorrow."

Marc places the novel on the dresser and the *Grand Atlas* next to the bed.

When his father closes the door, Jean-Philippe opens his lamp, picks up the atlas, and admires the maps. He turns the pages carefully in order not to damage them. He's dazzled by so much beauty, each page displaying a work of art filled with colors and symbols. After a few minutes, he places the atlas next to his pillow and falls asleep, his arm resting on the world.

5.

BIG BROTHER IS WATCHING YOU

March 2010

Calmness reigns in the eighth-floor corridor, where the silence seems to demand whispers. A few nurses move swiftly from room to room, while the guard at the central station directs Jean-Philippe to room 817. He listens through the half-open door. Slowly, he pushes the door into the dimness of the room. His brother Felix looks up, immediately leaving his chair, and approaches him in a determined pace.

"Look, a *revenant*!" he says in a dry tone, referring to his brother as a ghost.

Jean-Philippe steps back into the corridor, pushed there by his brother. Felix gently closes the door and crosses his arms, like a security guard in front of a star's dressing room. He looks at him intensely.

"It's a joke! Come here, little brother." He laughs.

Jean-Philippe smiles to hide his discomfort. Felix, a former football player, possesses an imposing physique, whereas Jean-Philippe embodies all the traits of a younger sibling: six years his junior, fifteen centimeters shorter and thirty kilograms lighter, maybe even thirty-five. Jean-Philippe inherited the slim build of his mother's family, the Sullivans, whereas his brother takes after the Genests.

Felix has always had difficulty controlling sarcasm, which he uses without restraint. He takes Jean-Philippe in his arms to welcome him properly, patting him too hard on the back, and passes his hand over his head.

"You haven't had your hair cut?" He laughs again. "How long has it been since we saw each other?"

"In person, five years already."

"There are a lot of people who will be surprised to see you. You didn't get pretty." More laughter.

"Is Mom here?" asks Jean-Philippe in order to divert the subject.

"No. Dad still has a few hours to sleep. I told her to go back home so she can rest and eat a little. You know it's not easy for her."

"I know, I spoke to her this week. That's why I'm here."

"Over the past few months, it has become heavy. But with the two of us, it will be simpler. You know, I work full time, sometimes days, evenings, weekends. My hours change. The girls go to dancing classes or horseback riding lessons. Julie and I can't split up. While you were traveling the world and living it up, who did our parents call? Me, obviously!"

"That's not quite right," Jean-Philippe defends himself.

"I know, I know. But now, I have my hands full. I didn't mean to bump into you, but I'm glad you're here. It will free me a little."

"Exactly, go find Julie. I'm going to stay here until Mom comes back. You'll be able to take some time for yourself. We'll have the opportunity to recoup lost time! How does that sound?"

"I won't say no to that. And if you insist, I'll take you up on your offer and go home to rest. Have you picked up an accent? Have you become British now?"

Jean-Philippe remembers being six years old, facing Felix, who was twice his age. Felix had locked him in the laundry basket, threatening him. "If you tell Mom that it was me who put you there, next time, it's going to be worse!"

Michelle took him out of the basket and punished him for his nonsense. He ended up in his room until the next day, without dessert—the worst punishment in the world. Looking back, even if he'd reported his brother, Michelle wouldn't have believed him. He had more energy than Felix. He constantly squirmed in his chair and got up during meals. He ran, climbed everywhere, and talked non-stop. Michelle threatened to tie him to his chair. She finally accepted that Jean-Philippe eat on his knees in his seat without getting up, an acceptable compromise under the circumstances.

Felix assumed the role of a third parent, constantly telling on him and pointing out his faults, whereas Jean-Philippe especially needed a caring big brother. He'd never succeeded in establishing a meaningful sibling relationship. It seemed that since his birth, Felix had become jealous of the attention he received, especially since Jean-Philippe demanded a lot of attention.

Felix now works as a police officer in the northern suburbs of Montreal—a perfect fit for a man who operates within a framework of norms and laws. As the eldest, Felix proclaimed himself the custodian of the family rules, which led to some misunderstandings and discomfort as he grew up. Michelle had to intervene with Felix so that he stopped reporting everything.

Whether in society or within the family, Felix consistently emphasized to his younger brother the importance of following the rules. As a big brother, he paved the way for him and wanted his little brother to follow the path. But Jean-Philippe was thinking outside the box, and Felix couldn't tolerate that he didn't follow in his footsteps. He observed him and reported his misbehavior to their parents.

Do you remember that: "Take an example from your brother," "Your brother would never have done that," "Felix didn't do things like that."

Felix excelled in all sports. The whole family attended college football games, and his team regularly won championships. His room was filled with trophies and medals. For his part, Jean-Philippe hated team sports and much preferred his bike. More intellectual and more creative, he invented stories and different universes, which had less impact in the community of Ithaca-on-the-Lake. When neighbors came to the house to greet the champion, Jean-Philippe remained in the shadows.

Now alone in the hospital room, he leaves his backpack and suitcase at the entrance. His father is sleeping to the rhythm of the monitor beeping at regular intervals. Standing at the foot of the bed, Jean-Philippe looks at his father lying there. He notices his father's thin face, the wrinkles that have invaded his skin, and how his once black hair is now more white than gray.

The memories pass through his head like a movie in fast forward: the birthday cakes, the book pages, the bicycle, the neighbors, the bursts of laughter, the fears and the tears, the quarrels and the silences. He sits on the bedside and gently takes his father's hand without moving it too much. His own hand is so small compared to Marc's.

"I came back," murmurs Jean-Philippe. "I've taken the first step. Now we have to talk. For real."

Blah, blah, blah! Not even able to say what you're thinking. Even when asleep, he scares you! Big coward!

He sits in the corner chair, waiting for his father to wake up. Peacefully, Jean-Philippe daydreams in the corner of the room. The dimness accentuates the drowsiness he struggles against. In the wall of his mind's bedroom, Jean-Philippe fixates on the image of his brother holding him by the neck, mimicking a wrestling hold.

At the age of eight, life is mostly carefree, except when it comes to anything related to someone named Felix. Every evening after supper, the boys stick to their routine: they start with homework, then Jean-Philippe spends thirty minutes listening to television before showering and going to bed. Being older, Felix has earned the privilege of going to bed later.

One evening, after stepping out of the shower, Jean-Philippe wraps a towel around his small body and another over his head, mimicking how women do it in movies. He holds the hairbrush in his hand like a microphone and sings at the top of his lungs. He spent the previous half hour doing like the "cool kids" at school did and listening to music videos on Much Music. In the bathroom, he continues to sing the title "Girls Just Want to Have Fun," because when he was eight, it was the most English he could pronounce.

Felix knocks on the door to take a shower, but Jean-Philippe, aiming to annoy his brother, sings even louder. With each knock from Felix, Jean-Philippe raises his voice more. Eventually, Felix complains to their mother to get Jean-Philippe to stop. As he hears her approaching, he unlocks the door to avoid confronting his mother. Felix rushes in, shoving him, and the younger brother finds himself on the floor.

"What are you doing with that on your head? You're not a girl!" Felix shouts, pulling on the towel.

"Stop! I didn't do anything to you!" Jean-Philippe defends himself.

"You're hanging out in the bathroom! Stop being selfish! We shouldn't have to wait until after 'the star' finishes his show!"

"Get up and go get dressed in your room," Michelle orders in the chaos of the bathroom.

"Jean-Philippe used two towels," denounces Felix.

"You're not the one doing the laundry! One towel is enough. I'm not your servant, I'm your mother. You should remember that," she reproaches him.

"The song was stuck in my head, and I couldn't help but sing it. Cyndi Lauper is so good!"

"If television excites you that much, I'll cut it off for you. It won't be long."

Marc comes into Jean-Philippe's room and sits at the foot of the bed. Evening speeches carry a much more solemn tone compared to the novel readings.

"There is a time to have fun and another to relax, and before bed, it's not a time to get excited," Marc lectures.

Music, even rock music, helps him sleep. Not like the candy his mother had quickly cut out for him. The consequences imposed by his mother tend to hurt rather badly. She knows how to use discipline to bring Jean-Philippe back on the right path. With all his hyperactivity, Michelle's threats remain very present in his mind.

"Take an example from your brother. He plays hockey with his friends, but he comes home early to do his homework. He watches television. He takes a shower and goes to bed. I have nothing to reproach him for," declares Marc.

"But he hits me all the time," complains Jean- Philippe.

"Between brothers, that's normal. You're going to have to toughen up. Life isn't always fun. We all have commitments. You're going to see it when you have a family. You have to make sacrifices in life. Look at us; we've decided for your mother to stay at home with both of you instead of working, which means we can't go to restaurants very often. That's life. You have to make choices," he explains.

Jean-Philippe doesn't want to imitate his brother. He hates sports and prefers to draw, build snow forts, or sing. He rarely finishes his projects, but he enjoys lots of activities, as long as his brother doesn't torment him. Caught between his dreams and the expectations of him, he sees a future he doesn't want. Sacrifices, always sacrifices, he who aims to change the world!

One day, Marc signs his youngest son up for hockey lessons, but Jean-Philippe spends the hour skating around the ice, holding his stick for support and playing with the puck. On their way out of the arena, when the figure skating group takes possession of the ice, Jean-Philippe jealously admires the skaters performing their pirouettes and jumps.

"It's almost like gymnastics. I'm sure I'd be good."

"I'm not going to spend an hour watching children skating in circles!" says his father.

Jean-Philippe never knows if his father is talking about figure skating or the past hour of hockey. But one thing is certain: he ends his hockey career the same day it begins.

6.

ROCKY ROAD

March 2010

Marc wakes up and mumbles a few words.

"It's 7:30 p.m.," Jean-Philippe replies, decoding that he wants to know the time.

"Felix?" he whispers.

"No. It's Jean-Philippe," he says, moving closer. He stands up and places his hand on his father's.

Marc sobs. In slow motion, he raises his other arm to hide his eyes, out of modesty.

"Take your time," Jean-Philippe reassures him.

Marc tries to speak through the tears. "I didn't want to have the operation without seeing you," he whispers.

"I'm here. We'll have time to talk."

Marc squeezes his son's fingers in his hand despite his lack of energy.

"I'm sorry. I'm sorry. I'm sorry," he repeats. "I thought I'd lost you forever." He continues to hold Jean-Philippe's hand as if to keep him there.

Jean-Philippe stands next to him until he falls back asleep under the effects of the morphine drip.

1987

Jean-Philippe enters the room of his memories and smiles. He's holding a photo of his first-grade class.

At the end of the afternoon, in the schoolyard, Daniel, Jessica, and Jean-Philippe are having fun in the sandbox recreating a village. Daniel installs pieces of wood to build a bridge for the small cars, Jean-Philippe digs a trench to simulate a river, and Jessica, for her part, plants flowers to enhance the make-believe city. Kevin, a fifth-grader, steps forward and crushes the little cars in the sand with his heel. He pushes Daniel and spits on Jessica. Despite reaching only the shoulders of the demolition man, Jean-Philippe stands up to put an end to the carnage. Kevin tells him to shut up and punches him in the face. Frightened, he falls to the ground and runs home, crying. With his eye swollen, he can no longer see clearly, and the left side of his face is in pain. He worries about his loss of vision, but also about his friends, Jessica and Daniel.

Marc gets angry and hits the wooden table with his big hand and it splits. "Attacking children who are playing. What kind of world do we live in?" he fumes.

He struggles to tolerate assaults, particularly on children, especially since they were having harmless fun. As a pacifist, he rejects violence to resolve conflicts and educates his sons according to this ideology. In Ithaca-on-the-Lake, where everyone in the village knows each other, Marc asks Jean-Philippe for the name of the fifth grader. He then takes the car keys to visit the young boy's parents' house.

"This is unacceptable," he repeats as he leaves the house.

An hour later, he informs the entire family that the issue with this individual will no longer cause any trouble for anyone.

The next day at school, everyone wants to see his black eye, but Jean-Philippe prefers not to discuss it. His face is transformed into an abstract work: his cheekbone is swollen and the outline of his eye is colored up to the eyebrow. He sees Kevin enter the courtyard, his eye swollen and marks on his face. Jean-Philippe wonders if Marc might have been responsible for the beating and if his father intended to seek revenge on his behalf.

Since then, the fifth grader has attacked other children in the playground but has no longer gone near the younger ones' section. He never bothers them again. During the school year, he even disappears. A rumor circulates in the village that Kevin now lives with a foster family and that his father risks prison because he was violent. When he looks at his father, Jean-Philippe finds it difficult to imagine that a man would beat his own children.

"To hit someone is to take away their dignity," Marc preaches.

7.

ONE EARTHQUAKE PER DAY

March 2010

When Michelle enters Marc's room, she rushes toward Jean-Philippe, whom she hasn't held in her arms for five long years. She holds him tightly against her, to prevent him from getting away. If it were up to Michelle, her son would never leave the family home again.

"I'm going to stay until Dad gets back on his feet. I'll be here as long as necessary," says Jean-Philippe.

It's only following this promise that Michelle agrees to release her son from her embrace.

"Don't ever do that to me again!" she reprimands him.

The relationship between a mother and her son is an unbreakable bond. Jean-Philippe could have committed murder or decided to get into pornography, and she would love him just as much. Of course, she has her mood swings and sometimes reacts intensely. Michelle blames herself for past mistakes. After all, the apple doesn't fall far from the tree.

She loves Jean-Philippe as much as Felix, but Michelle had such difficulty having a second child that an indelible bond unites them.

July 1989

On July 10th, Jean-Philippe's life takes an unexpected trajectory. Like Phileas Fogg and Jean Passepartout in *Around the World in Eighty Days*, he's convinced that explorations will be at the heart of his existence! This revelation ignites in him a feeling of euphoria. He radiates and holds this certainty like King Arthur pulling Excalibur from the rock.

In the early afternoon, as the sun and heat begin to subside, Michelle sends the two brothers outside to play.

"The weather is too good to stay inside. Go out! I don't want the two of you to get in my way," she decrees.

She undertakes to turn the living room around—one of her expressions. She rushes to revamp the room before the start of her soap operas. For several days, the sunlight reflecting on the television screen has hindered Michelle's ability to fully appreciate the trials and tribulations of rich American families in the afternoon soap operas. So, several times a year, she reorganizes not only the living room but also the other rooms in the house, motivated both by necessity and the desire to impart a sense of novelty. Like a designer, Michelle uses creativity. She switches some frames and changes the shelf trinkets. Some plants are promoted to the edge of the bay window while others are relocated to the kitchen.

Michelle's inventiveness extends to several aspects of family life: food, sewing, and even hairdressing. Innovation rescues her from the monotony of routine. Nothing for dinner? No problem. Simply cook slices of bologna in a pan; as they curl, they'll take the shape of bowler hats and, when paired with a touch of ketchup, they resemble sombreros. The children never go without food, and occasionally, the novelty is such a hit that they prefer it over a traditional meal.

Every Halloween, Michelle enjoys crafting her sons' costumes: using the bottom of a bleach bottle as a headpiece, she transforms Jean-Philippe into an alien. Her imagination knows no bounds; she was repurposing materials long before it became a trend.

That afternoon, Michelle asks Felix to look after Jean-Philippe. For a teenager, this is the ultimate torture. At fifteen, he would have preferred playing hockey in the street or tossing a football with his friends rather than staying with his younger brother. What a drag! Consequently, Felix instructs his little brother to remain in the courtyard, gets on his bike, and leaves Jean-Philippe alone on the steps.

"I'm going to tell Mom that you won't play with me," Jean-Philippe shouts to Felix.

"If you say anything, I'll lock you in the safe in the basement," Felix threatens, foot on the pedal, prepared to depart once more.

Alone, Jean-Philippe ponders for a few minutes. He realizes that he hasn't used the old swing and the sandbox in the yard for a year. At nine years old, he considers himself too grown-up for games meant for younger children.

In his reflection, he recalls the excerpt from *Around the World in Eighty Days* that his father read the day before.

> Unhappily for his master, as well as himself, his curiosity drew him unconsciously farther off than he intended to go. At last, having seen the Parsee carnival wind away in the distance, he was turning his steps toward the station, when he happened to espy the splendid pagoda on Malabar Hill, and was seized with an irresistible desire to see its interior. He was quite ignorant that it is forbidden to Christians to enter certain Indian temples, and that even the faithful must not go in without first leaving their shoes outside the door. It may be said here that the wise policy of the British Government severely punishes a disregard of the practices of the native religions.

Jean-Philippe then makes a significant decision that will alter his young life. He reasons that if Felix can visit his friends, he's also capable of doing the same. Despite living on the other side of the village, he considers himself old enough to go to Daniel's house. However, the railway, which divides the town in two, serves as a forbidden boundary. Even so, Jean-Philippe is well aware of the concept of caution and is adept at showing it. With the flashing lights, sounds, and vibrations, anyone would be reckless not to notice the oncoming train.

He hops on his bicycle and roams around the familiar neighborhood of Ithaca-on-the-Lake, where the small wooden church, the Pleiades primary school, the town hall, and the municipal library are situated. The grocery store and bakery are lined up along Main Street, near the river. Also, there's Nestor's Snack Bar, which offers the best hot dogs in the world, especially when the owner adds paprika on top. He takes detours to go to the baker's window and admire the mochas and palm hearts that make him salivate. Jean-Philippe's fondness for pastries is nothing new.

He finally sets out to climb the mound at the top of which the railway is situated. He applies the brakes in front of the rails and gazes at the unexplored territory ahead. In his neighborhood, residents don't see the new area because of the elevation of the railway line. He hesitates to take the step that will lead him to the new region. The unknown fascinates him. He looks both ways. There's no indication of an impending train arrival. His desire to discover, to push boundaries, and to live experiences is at its peak.

He crosses the unauthorized border and lets his bicycle roll to the bottom of the mound. He pedals with confidence, ready to face his destiny. His heart beating hard, every muscle in his legs gains power with each turn of the pedals. He stands straight, head held high like a lioness searching for a prey. He rides on full of nobility, with the wind at his back.

In the new district, the architecture stands out with its houses whose brick and aluminum facings replace the wood which predominates in old Ithaca. In the car with his parents, Jean-Philippe has already traveled across the new Ithaca to reach the soccer field where the St. John the Baptist Day—the national holiday—fireworks display was held. He paid little attention to the surroundings, especially since it was dark, and his focus was directed toward the vibrant colors in the sky.

For his first solo visit, he sets off in search of Daniel's home. He knows that his friend lives near the municipal swimming pool, without more information. He bikes along the baseball field, where an employee is busy maintaining the surface for the evening's games. Large, metal poles supporting dozens of spotlights surround the grassy area. Stands placed behind each players' bench await spectators ready to encourage their favorite athletes.

Jean-Philippe visualizes every detail of the landscape to refine his observation skills and evolve into a better explorer.

Thanks to the precision of his orientation skills, he can easily locate himself, preventing him from going in circles. As he turns the corner, he sees the swimming pool crowded with young boys and girls. He hears the high-pitched voices, which increase in decibels when he approaches. He even inhales the disinfectant odor of chlorine. Among the dozens of bathers, he identifies three children who were classmates with him during the previous school year.

Jean-Philippe continues on his way and sees Daniel outside his house with his parents. They're getting ready to leave for their cottage in the north.

Surprised to see him, Daniel is especially impressed by his recent acquisition. "Is that your new bike?" he asks.

"Yes, it's a gift. The other was too small. My father gave it to my cousin."

"The color is incredible! When I come back from the cottage, we'll go for a ride."

"Are you going away for a long time?"

"We'll be there for two weeks. I'll call you when I get back," he promises.

Daniel has always been Jean-Philippe's best friend. One day, he would like to go to the cabin with Daniel if his parents allow it. He could climb trees or engage in archeological digs. Jean-Philippe's parents cannot afford to buy a cottage. For them, an outdoor vacation means going for a drive in the mountains and coming back to sleep at home. Of course, a day sitting next to Felix doesn't make for the best vacation.

He resumes his route and follows part of the Telemachus River, which supplies the village with drinking water. The stream takes its source at the St. Penelope reservoir in the north, curving through the countryside before reaching Ithaca-on-the-Lake and ultimately flowing toward the St. Lawrence River. Jean-Philippe envies the father and his son fishing on the shore.

Winding through the various streets, Jean-Philippe finds himself at the new, freshly landscaped park. He stops his bike close to the swings, noticing that one of the seats is rolled up onto the crossbar. He rotates the large roundabout and attempts to climb onto it. Unfortunately, the rapid spinning of the large metal plate causes him to inevitably slide off. This maneuver needs another person, and he promises himself he'll come back with Daniel. He explores the area filled with large, concrete cylinders of all colors, on which he climbs until he stands atop them.

In his mind, Jean-Philippe visualizes himself delving into the underground sewers of a metropolis, facing mutant creatures transformed by the chemical runoffs from surface industries. He constructs a mental image of a rocket that launches on a journey toward an unfamiliar planet. There, he envisions harvesting plants to design innovative drugs. Eventually, he gathers valuable archeological artifacts and defends himself and his campsite against attacking bandits. He clings to the concrete pipe's wall, careful to evade the flowing lava below. His adventures are both exciting and terrifying.

Following these stimulating experiences, Jean-Philippe rides his bicycle back home. His stomach is growling, and he intends to approach his mother and ask for some cookies, hoping she'll accept.

Phileas Fogg had adventures as thrilling as Jean-Philippe's, but they don't share the same mother. And Jean-Philippe has to abstain from cookies for several days. It's a distressed woman who greets him, a mother in a panic whose cries echo those of the young girls at the swimming pool.

"Where have you been? Do you know what time it is? What did I tell you? Do you know what I went through? I sent your brother and your father looking for you everywhere! What was going through your mind? What the hell were you thinking? It doesn't make sense to make me experience emotions like that!" shouts Michelle.

She expresses her worry by speaking very quickly. Obviously, Jean-Philippe knows the answer to several of his mother's questions, but his brain tells him to remain silent for his own safety. With all his adventures, he lost track of time and forgot it was time for supper. Noticing the absence of her youngest son, Michelle sent Felix and Marc to look for him, and they set off into the village in opposite directions.

"I thought about calling the police! Do you understand that this is serious? If something were to happen..." she says without completing the sentence for fear of hearing herself say the unacceptable.

Jean-Philippe remains silent. He stares at the floor, avoiding meeting the gaze of his mother, who has surely developed the skill of transforming him into a rock-like Medusa, or worse.

Felix enters the kitchen.

"I told you to stay in the courtyard. You didn't listen to me, and you upset Mom!" he declares arrogantly.

"If something had happened to you, I wouldn't have recovered! It's terrible! All the things I thought about. I thought you were kidnapped! Do you know what that means?" Michelle replies on the verge of tears.

His mother's panic attacks always progress in the same way: at the beginning, it's anger and questions, followed by guilt which she projects onto her son, to finally end with consequences.

"You're going to take a bath. Afterward, you'll go to bed," she insists.

Jean-Philippe heads toward his room, suppressing a smile because, despite everything, he had a memorable day. Curiosity got the better of him, but he feels blessed to have finally glimpsed his destiny: to travel around the world like Phileas Fogg, even if for the moment, he'll only be exploring his room.

He's used to messing up. How can he make his parents understand that he has found his passion? They would respond that he had time to change ideas, that like always, he typically moves from one interest to another without pushing further.

How many times did he insist on learning the guitar, the violin, the piano? He constantly changes, lacks focus, and his impulsiveness is ten times more pronounced.

You will never be strong enough. It's already lost. You should let it go.

However, on July 10th, Jean-Philippe really wants to be like Phileas Fogg. Maybe by focusing on that, he can get there.

Marc enters the room with a sandwich and sits at the foot of the bed. His stomach gurgling, Jean-Philippe gulps down the sandwich and refrains from speaking. He doesn't want to spend his summer vacation between the four walls of his room.

"Your mother prepared this for you. She wouldn't want you to be sick tonight. Eat first, then I'll turn off the light, and I don't want to hear anything afterward. No reading tonight. I want you to think about what you put us through today. I don't know if you realize what happened. I thought you had more common sense than that. I thought I'd lost you! You disappointed me a lot today. I want you to think about that tonight."

No common sense, big disappointment…

Every word sinks into his head. Jean-Philippe never wanted to disappoint his parents, because disappointment affects him terribly.

After Felix's birth, Michelle suffered two miscarriages. She had to wait several years before becoming pregnant again. She made many sacrifices before Jean-Philippe's birth to avoid any risk and bring the pregnancy to term. The long-awaited baby was finally born, the miracle child who carried with him all the pressure and hopes of his parents.

March 2010

Michelle watches her son sleeping in the hospital chair. The effects of jet lag have gotten the better of him. Standing between her husband and her son, her two men asleep, she doesn't want to disturb their sleep. Jean-Philippe's return was a delight, a joy similar to what she'd felt at his birth. Unconsciously, the last five years felt like the time of miscarriages, mishaps, and failed attempts at pregnancy.

Each phone call she made once a month reminded her of the words she spoke to him when Jean-Philippe was in her womb. The return of her son is, in a sense, a rebirth

8.

THE ORIGIN OF WORDS

March 2010

The hospital room is filled with flowers, stuffed animals, and cards. The number of gifts confirms the appreciation of the citizens of Ithaca-on-the-Lake for their mayor. From home, Michelle has brought his bathrobe, a blanket, and games of all kinds to pass the time when his condition allows it. Jean-Philippe and Michelle stay at the hospital for a few hours a day, especially at the start of the day when visits are sparse.

"Have you moved into your old room?" Marc asks. "Did you see we put your bed back? It makes a place for Camille and Charlie when they come to sleep at home."

"Do you read them stories like when I was younger?" questions Jean-Philippe.

"No. They don't have the same interests as you. They mostly like dancing. Did you know that Camille takes horseback riding lessons?"

"Felix may have told me something about it..."

"They're so adorable," he says kindly.

"I don't know where they got that quality. Julie, I imagine!" proposes Jean-Philippe.

"Don't say that," Michelle replies. "Your brother is a good father to the girls. You didn't have much affinity, especially with the age gap. It was difficult for you, as it was for him."

"Age is one thing, but we were so different! Above all, I was too much for him. He had to take care of me, and he didn't want to do it. I was a burden, and he made me feel like it. Afterward, he moved into an apartment and when he came to see you from time to time, it was as if I didn't exist."

"You're exaggerating a little, aren't you?"

"I say it sincerely. Don't get me wrong. I know I wasn't relaxing for you! My God, I must have puzzled you. I lacked common sense. I told countless lies! However, most of the time, I was in my own universe—a new planet or a jungle! Remember? I used to draw treasure maps and search for pirate ships, just like in *The Goonies* movie! I was a Goony, and I really believed myself!"

Throughout his childhood, maps fascinated Jean-Philippe. He created them, drew them, admired them. Each map told a story, and each atlas, a novel. When he was very young, he read pages of the atlas, articulating the names of cities with the accent of the country. Even though his German and Russian accents sounded the same, he ranted through the house about the Vladivostok, Dnipropetrovsk, and Düsseldorf he'd just read. He explored world maps like a navigator. He imagined himself on expeditions filled with conquests and loots.

"When we weren't pirates, we were spies. At Daniel's house, you remember, we collected tomatoes behind his house; we hid and threw them at the cars like grenades. You reprimanded us, and I remember telling you that there was a secret agent in the car and that we were hired to install detectors to track vehicles. You threatened to wash my tongue out with soap if I told lies again. I had fun in my world! You must have laughed at my whims from time to time?" he asks.

"We remember it," says Marc. "We never knew what you were going to do next. You surely entertained us!"

"But now you have your granddaughters to keep you young."

"Camille and Charlie, they're the only grandchildren we're going to have, so we're taking care of them."

A score of one to zero for Dad! In any case, you're not going to have children with Rahim!

Jean-Philippe takes a deep breath and withholds his reply. He adores his nieces like his own daughters, even from a distance. Out the corner of her eye, Michelle detects the discomfort and while continuing her knitting, adds,

"You could adopt or hire a surrogate mother. There are a lot of men who have children today. I saw this on television."

"I don't think that's a good idea. I travel all over the world with impossible schedules. I'm at peace with the fact that I won't have children, and I'm more than happy with that. I have no regrets or doubts."

"If you're happy with that, that's the main thing," says Michelle.

"Weren't you only supposed to stay in London for a year?" Marc asks.

"Yes, it's true. The program was planned for one year, but I was offered another contract, thanks to Jerry."

"Jerry?"

"My mentor. All new reporters are paired with an experienced journalist for the first year, like an internship. I followed him all over the world, visiting unexpected places while learning the trade. We went from barely inhabited islands to deep in a jungle. It was astonishing. Even now, I call him regularly for advice or when I have doubts about an article. He shared with me the 'tricks of the trade,' as he called them, and he became like a second father to me."

Marc emits a cry of pain as he moves in the bed.

One-one! It's a draw!

Jean-Philippe learned the ropes of the profession thanks to this experienced journalist. This little man with the big mustache yellowed by cigarettes has been writing in the *World Compass* for more than twenty-five years and has traveled around the world more than once. Jerry supported him in taking risks, both in writing reports and in the field.

"Jerry would often sit at a café, smoking his cigarette, and let me conduct interviews. Upon my return, he'd inquire about my findings. Then, he would say, 'My boy'—that's what he called me—'it wasn't a great day; we'll start again tomorrow! Did you at least find a good restaurant?' Jean-Philippe chuckles. "Imagine the scene. One day, sitting on a terrace in Warsaw, he listened to passersby and keenly observed them. Though he didn't know Polish, by interpreting intonation, word variations, and gestures, he initiated conversations on their day, politics, or news. Bam! He could craft a two thousand-word article. It's more nuance, though. All in all, my mentor wields words gracefully, with refinement, yet a hint of sharpness. I've learned that for a journalist, ears sometimes outweigh intellect. Sensitivity is key."

Is this a message for your father?

Jerry encouraged him to use different figures of speech in his texts, to dare to talk about his personal experiences, and to ask surprising yet unconventional questions during his field meetings. Surprises and discomfort provoke confidences and consequently enhance the quality of the texts. Jerry taught him how to stand out in the world of publishing, a rather competitive environment. He took his protege under his wing with kind criticism and co-signed the articles out of obligation, while giving Jean-Philippe the credit in front of the bosses.

"I worked seventy, even eighty hours a week perfecting my texts. I was learning to use more English expressions and move away from French sentence structures. I was good in English, but it's not my mother tongue, so I had to learn the intricacies of Shakespeare's language. Jerry said, 'Style is more important than spelling.' "

Jerry quickly noticed Jean-Philippe's potential and recommended him to publishers for the renewal of his contract. In his recommendation, he wrote that the Quebecer possessed a style and a point of view that transcended challenges with written language. Jean-Philippe demonstrated an impeccable work ethic, prompting Jerry to state that he was ready for independent reporting.

"We were only two interns to see our contract renewed for a second year. I was both proud and torn."

"What for? It was a great opportunity, wasn't it?" asks Michelle.

"Exactly, but I found myself at a crossroads. To the left was the choice to return to Quebec and begin anew, while to the right was the path of involvement with the *World Compass*, which meant I would have to stay in London for several years."

"And you decided to stay in London," says Marc with a touch of sadness.

"I no longer had anything tying me to Montreal. I decided to pursue my dream, and nothing and no one could deter me."

Two to one! Match point: Jean-Philippe. Considering a boy who doubts everything, I find your certainty somewhat lacking.

Jean-Philippe rises from the small, blue metal chair and moves around to wake his numb body.

"I've built myself a life in London, with extraordinary friends. I write in a magazine that has a circulation of more than a million copies. Can you imagine how many people read me all over the world?"

Michelle gets up and mentions that she's going to the cafeteria to get some coffee. Jean-Philippe tells her that he has water left in his bottle. Finally alone with Marc, he shakes his t-shirt to release the heat that is accumulating inside him. His ears ring, and his face flushes.

“You know why I came back, right?” he asks his father.

“Yes, I know. But there's no point in revisiting old stories. What matters most is to focus on the future. I don't understand why we often dwell on the past when our focus should be on what lies ahead.”

“Anyway, we haven't spoken in five years. Don't you think we should at least get some closure on the subject?”

“What happened back then is done and dusted. It's not difficult to comprehend,” Marc says in a dry tone.

“But still—”

“I'm not asking you to apologize. Everybody makes mistakes. The fact that you’re here shows me that water has flowed under the bridge.”

Jean-Philippe's sighs attest to his impatience.

“That's not quite how I see it. This proves that we should talk about it,” he says, looking at his father.

A sudden intense pain interrupts the conversation. Marc places his hand on his stomach and closes his eyes.

You’re killing your father with your questions.

“Do you want me to go and find someone?” he asks, rising, prepared to hurry to the nurses' station.

“No, it’ll pass. It's already getting better. It comes and goes.”

“Take slow breaths. You’re less red now. Would you like some water?”

“No, thanks. I hope the next crisis will be less painful. One day at a time, as they say. We learn to move forward, just like in family stories. Nobody’s perfect, but it’s important to keep looking ahead.”

"It's not insignificant, what happened," says Jean-Philippe, trying to steer the conversation back to the reason for his return.

"Stop it, Jean-Philippe! You're back, and that's the most important thing right now. Don't ruin your mother's happiness by thinking about the negative. We'll do ourselves more harm than good by going back to the past. It's unhealthy."

Staring at the floor, Jean-Philippe can't help but wonder if his father is right. Why does he always have to look into his past? Why has he retained his feelings of anger all these years? Was it easier to forget? Simple, yes. Easy, no. He has a trunk full of memories to prove it.

Where is the confrontation you promised yourself? Did you return it to the drawer?

Marc's friends and extended family take advantage of weekday evenings to visit him in the hospital. Furthermore, even though a memo was sent to the municipality, certain councilors come to meet Marc in his room. At first glance, they've come to check on him, but after a few minutes, the discussion inevitably turns to politics. Michelle attempts to impose a truce on the subject, without success.

Felix takes over from Jean-Philippe and his mother when his schedule allows it. Naturally, Jean-Philippe finds himself keeping his father company during the day, because writing isn't a job, according to Felix.

"What does your new column talk about?" asks his father. "Is it about travels?"

"Actually, it's about geography and legends. What interests me the most are the links between geology and mythology."

"Mythology? Like the Greek gods?" asks Michelle.

"In the past, people often didn't have the scientific background to interpret occurrences. Phenomena like volcanoes, for instance, were commonly narrated through legends or tales, and these stories have persisted across centuries. What I aim to communicate to my readers is the translation of oral traditions from these cultures on written pages. For instance, storytellers will explain the shape of a rock through the story about a witch who turned a person into stone. It's a typical story in several societies.

"Sometimes, they teach their children specific dangers by creating a monster. By scaring them, they hope their children won't venture into forbidden areas, achieving their objective in a certain way. This gives you an idea of the type of article I write. Also, I try to connect the legend to our daily lives, bridging ancient tales to contemporary experiences."

"That's an interesting way to discover new facets of the world," admits Marc.

"The Mythographers—that's the title of my column— are people who have been collecting myths for centuries. It's inspired by a book found in the Vatican, written during the Middle Ages, that brings together the myths of Greek and Roman antiquity."

"That's old!" says Michelle.

"Myths cover a wide array of subjects, including psychology, among others. I select legends that are connected to geology, involving rocks, topographical features, geographical phenomena, and then document them in writing. My goal is to explore this visual and historical richness. It's infinite, because each culture has their unique set of legends."

"You'll be able to write a lot of articles!" Michelle exclaims with admiration.

"In the *World Compass*, it spans across four pages, with photos taken by Amy. It's not very long, so I have to be concise yet impactful. Presently, I've been allocated five columns, and later, we'll assess whether we continue or not."

Jean-Philippe stretches his back muscles by rotating his pelvis and pulling his arms above his head, while twisting his torso from one side to the other.

"You haven't changed," observes Marc. "Do you always need to move?"

"I can't sit still for too long. I get up, I walk, I run. It allows me to concentrate. I do this at the office too."

"Who's Amy?" asks Michelle. "Is this your photographer colleague?"

"Yes. Well, she's more than my colleague. She's my friend, my partner in crime! She's the sister I never had. Over time, Amy has become my pillar, my confidante, the one who grounds me."

"I hope you take care of her! Friends are important in life."

Jean-Philippe chuckles. He recalls all the pranks he's played on her over the past four years.

"Let's just say I've played a few tricks on her, and in turn, I've been her victim several times!"

Amy grumbles as she enters Postojna Cave in Slovenia. She holds her bag containing her camera and Jean-Philippe carries the tripod.

"Why did you choose this place? You know I hate caverns."

"A cave beneath a castle. Maybe we'll see dragons. There's something to dream about. Besides, it's an opportunity to confront your fears. It's like therapy."

"Therapy, my ass!" she says as she looks at every corner of the cave for bats.

"Miss Cromarty! You shouldn't say bad words!" Jean-Philippe laughs.

"Fuck you, JeanPea!"

She moves slowly, lifting each foot carefully. She examines her boots to see if droppings from those flying rats have stuck to her feet.

"It's humid! It smells bad," she complains.

"Follow me. I'll guide you."

"If you see one of those critters, you warn me. I don't like them!"

Amy walks behind her colleague, head bowed, her fishing hat pulled tightly over her ears. Smaller in stature than Jean-Philippe, she holds onto her friend by the belt.

As he enters a new room in the cavern, he suddenly stops. He looks around and starts shouting:

"Look out!"

Without hesitation, Amy throws herself on the ground, hands on her head. Standing upright next to her, Jean-Philippe smiles with malicious pleasure. He helps her get up.

"Is it gone?" she asks.

"I think it was simply a stone falling from the ceiling. We narrowly escaped," he said, exaggerating his words.

At the second warning, Amy starts to suspect that Jean-Philippe is teasing her. Her pants and hands are stained with mud and bat guano.

Upon entering the wide "concert hall," they encounter acoustics that cast a magical aura. The ambient music reverberates against every wall, creating a deep and mysterious sound that fills the space. Once more, Jean-Philippe shouts a bat alert, prompting Amy to swiftly drop to the ground. This time, as she falls, she hits her knee, causing a sharp pain in her joint. Jean-Philippe bursts into laughter, oblivious to any actual presence of bats since the beginning.

"Stop laughing! I'll never trust you again!"

"I'm truly sorry," Jean-Philippe says amid snickers.

"I can see that. Tell it to your face! Quit teasing and lend me a hand to sit up," she commands.

Jean-Philippe assists her in reaching the bench in the concert hall. As Amy catches her breath, he leaves the tripod next to her and begins to explore the theater surrounded by natural limestone columns.

He walks alone in the center of the vast hall. An aria from Tchaikovsky's *Swan Lake* fills the gallery and transports him to another era. He attempts a few ballet steps, lacking both experience and talent. In his own world, he embodies Prince Siegfried in pursuit of his beautiful Odette. With the grace of Nureyev, although wearing bulky hiking shoes, Jean-Philippe improvises choreographies, easily managing to go on point with his rigid soles.

March 2010

Jean-Philippe takes a seat again after acting out the anecdote from the Slovenian cave.

"Believe it or not, Amy managed to get her revenge. Unbeknownst to me, she took a photo of me, and the image ended up becoming my journalist profile in the *World Compass*. It was printed in thousands of copies. Usually, reporters have their facial portraits. In my case, I'm striking an arabesque pose. Ever since, I've been nicknamed the 'Dancing Explorer,' and for my birthday last year, the magazine team enlarged the photo to poster size and presented it to me as a gift."

This photo, although funny, symbolizes his newfound freedom. Jean-Philippe has lived the best years of his life with Amy. He suffered from imposter syndrome for a long time and had difficulty accepting compliments. Always working harder to prove his worth, his importance, his place. Living with a saboteur and an imposter in his mind equates to facing life with two strikes against him. However, he never gave up and maintained his goal of becoming an explorer, as he'd promised his younger self.

When the publishers agreed to entrust him with the Mythographers column, he couldn't believe it. It was such a great opportunity for a young journalist. Yet they were betting on him, like a new racehorse. He hung the photo of the 'Dancing Explorer' in his living room to remember his colleagues' consideration of him. He had to stop discrediting himself and doubting. Kindness begins with oneself, and he had to constantly repeat this to himself.

"But you still do long reports?"

"Yes, I won't stop. Discovering new regions and engaging with people on-site is exhilarating. Human beings are full of stories ready to be told. When we delve into the lives of men and women, we witness how we share the same needs, the same dreams, the same aspirations, the same fears," relates Jean-Philippe as if he were delivering a speech in front of an attentive crowd.

"I recognize myself in them. When we extract the essence of goodness from every human being, we realize that we're all interconnected. The sorrow of a woman who loses her child transcends circumstances; it's a universal experience. Our expressions of grief vary, but the mourning persists. In the Western world, our focus is often inward. We must broaden our perspectives, embrace diversity, and comprehend our shared humanity."

"In Ithaca-on-the-Lake, we see Mexicans workers in the fields. It's amusing because I sometimes wonder what they think of us Quebecers," says Michelle.

"I think they actually come from Guatemala, those who work in our region," interjects Marc.

"The Mexicans from Guatemala—anyway, them—they probably find our setting peculiar. It might seem to them as if they've landed in the wrong place. They're nice and all, but surely they think it's chilly here," she adds. "And they're accustomed to the heat."

Jean-Philippe and Marc laugh at Michelle's slip of the tongue.

"Either they come from Mexico or Guatemala. Those are two different countries," says Jean-Philippe.

"You know I'm not good in geography. You don't get that passion from me. If you told me that France is at the end of the St. Lawrence River, I'd believe you. I still don't even understand daylight hours in one country while it's nighttime elsewhere," she says.

Jean-Philippe turns the chair, resting his arms in front of him on the backrest.

"You're making me dream. Do you remember when I read *Around the World in Eighty Days* to you? It was a bit like your first trip," says Marc, fond memories reflected in his eyes.

"It took months, or rather, years before we completed it because I asked so many questions. In fact, it was thanks to that novel that I wanted the career I have. Through Jules Verne, I discovered my adventurous spirit. He had a particular way of bringing together scientific elements in his stories. That's a bit like what I'm doing today. He was a great inspiration, and it was you, Dad, who introduced me to him. The evening was my favorite time of the day when you took time with me.

"There are books that impact us more than others. For me, it was *Around the World in Eighty Days*. I can't quite articulate it, but that novel brought about an awakening within me that significantly influenced my entire life. At first, I thought it was the world itself, the geography, that fascinated me. Yet in reality, it was the book as a symbolic object that truly captivated my interest. I understood the power of books, and that's what brought me to writing."

"Now, you're somewhat like the Jules Verne of the 21st century," says Marc.

"I hadn't quite envisioned it that way. I like the idea."

The Jules Verne of the poor! Do you think you have his talent?

"I want readers to embrace ownership of our world's heritage and recognize the profound richness it holds. There's an immense beauty inside every individual on Earth, often unnoticed, and my role is to illuminate it," he adds.

You're going to go blind from all those lights on you! Did your father say he was proud of you? I haven't heard it yet! What's the next step, becoming pope? Maybe he'd react then!

9.

A BEAM IN THE EYE

March 2010

Alone in the family home, Jean-Philippe stares at the blank screen of his laptop. Michelle spends her days at the hospital with her husband, and Jean-Philippe is taking advantage of his alone time to focus on finalizing the column due at the end of the week. Sitting at the kitchen table, he writes a part of a sentence and promptly erases it. Not a single word he types satisfies him. He leans back in the chair and crosses his arms, grumbling at his computer as if the device was the instigator of his lack of inspiration. Discouragement invades Jean-Philippe's body. In front of his screen, he bangs his forehead on the wood of the table, arms limp at his sides, emitting a mantra of despair from his throat.

Shifting his gaze, he notices the new curtains adorning the window above the sink. The microwave oven that occupies the end of the counter adjacent to the white fridge as well as the cabinet handles have been replaced. Other than these small details, the kitchen retains its familiar appearance, reminiscent of his childhood memories.

Sitting in the heart of his past, he struggles to attain the concentration he seeks. The surge of memories within this kitchen makes it challenging. He envisions himself once more at two years old, emptying the bottom of the cupboards filled with pots and plastic containers. At four, his father placed him on the counter to take his temperature during a bout of scarlet fever. At six, he sketched while standing on a chair before tumbling onto the linoleum. Today, he occupies the seat at the end of the table, the traditional spot once filled by his father, who, as the head of the family, always sat there.

He gets up, retrieves a plate from the cupboard, and grabs some utensils from the drawer. Instinctively, he finds everything he needs in the kitchen from another era. The furniture changes places, but the contents of the cabinets don't move. Every object is in its place. Jean-Philippe stands as the only outsider in this house.

He slices a square of brownie specially baked by his mother just for him. He places the small piece of cake in the center of his plate and observes it, so tiny in the middle of the dish, like an orphan. He hesitates to cut a larger piece, but opts to take two cookies from the jar before returning to sit in front of the computer screen.

What's happening? Are you out of inspiration? Have you lost your mojo? Do you miss your friends? Are you missing sex? You're lacking energy, aren't you?

Jean-Philippe retrieves his iPhone and dials his friend's number.

"JeanPea!" Amy shouts from the other end of the line. "So good to hear from you, my friend! How are you, old man?"

"Physically, I'm all right. I've gained some weight from the number of cookies my mother bakes. I guess I haven't been running as often as I should!"

"Stop it, your body's perfect! It'll do you good to have some flaws. I won't be the only one with curves," she says.

"Mentally, things could be better. I'm not at home and it's taking a toll. I'm in and out of the hospital just about every day. I'm trying to keep my spirits up, but I'm drained. I'm trying to write, but inspiration seems to elude me."

"Give yourself some time. Your mind is occupied with a lot, that's perfectly normal."

"I had a conversation with Mr. Forster, and he says I can continue to work remotely. He's read the first column and he's thrilled with it. I'm going to revise and update some old articles to fit the format of The Mythographers."

"That's excellent news. I knew we had something good."

"I've thought about writing a column on Quebec. You could come and take a look here?"

"Do you miss your girlfriend?" she teases him.

"I miss you and Rahim too. I haven't spoken to him in a while. We had an argument before I left. I wasn't very nice to him."

"Fortunately, you're not here in front of me, or I'd be speaking to you eye to eye! JeanPea, you have to get your head out of your ass. Rahim is a good guy, really nice, and he loves you! Do you understand this? *He loves you!* He sees you in his curry soup. You're his precious little butter chicken!"

"I know it."

"Say it to your head then. Do you want it to end between you two?"

"No, that's not it. What can I say? I'm like this. I doubt myself all the time, and I don't feel I'm good enough for him."

"He's mature enough to make his own decisions. Let him make his choices. You don't need to advocate for him. You've been together for two years, and you drool when you talk about him. If that's not love, you have overactive salivary glands!"

"He comes from an extremely wealthy family. I feel like a street kid next to him. Our backgrounds are so different. I come from a modest, traditional family that isn't well-off.

"Bullshit!"

I think I've heard that somewhere!

"Call him, it's urgent! If you were with me, I'd smack you upside the head!"

"Ouch! I think I felt that!"

"So much the better. It's what you deserve! Listen, I wouldn't have the same speech if he tried to change you by making you a housemaid. This isn't the case. He doesn't place himself above you. He respects you and he's open to what you have to say, and vice versa. I experienced it—the great love of my life—and I threw everything away for minor details. Don't repeat my mistakes; go for it. Trust me, I'll be there to put you back on track if you get lost."

Even on the other side of the ocean, her energy resonates, causing goosebumps on his skin. Jean-Philippe envies the artist, but above all, he deeply respects his friend. She serves as his lifeline in times of need, a safety net for his doubts, frankness during his uncertainties.

Amy's talent adds depth to Jean-Philippe's stories, and the magazine couldn't envision separating these two exceptional talents—a relationship evolving in trust, a perfect match. He embodies the faithful man she desires, her pillar of resilience. She becomes the sister and confidant he never had. Amy is the only person who has the ability to pass through the walls of his mind. Immune to Jean-Philippe's doubts, she takes great pleasure in stirring up his ideas.

As much as Jean-Philippe calmed Amy in her existential crises following her separation, Amy rocked Jean-Philippe when he mourned his loneliness. Too proud to talk about it, Amy knew that JeanPea missed Quebec. She took his tall body against her small shoulders. She would bring out the scotch and beer for an evening of vices and ending up singing "Sweet Dreams" at four in the morning. With a glass in hand and alcohol coursing through their veins, they seemed to sing more passionately about the world, the seven seas, and the nuances of use and abuse!

In 2006, when his contract was renewed, the editors of *World Compass* wanted to secure Jean-Philippe by providing him with the chance to collaborate with an accomplished photographer. Amy, a recipient of numerous prestigious international awards, had her photos featured in an exhibition in London and regularly published in monthly magazines such as *Time* and *Harper's Bazaar*.

"I miss you too!" she says tenderly. "I will definitely come see you. I, too, have a new project starting."

"You do? Tell me."

"As you know, the *World Compass* is expanding into book publishing. They've offered to publish an album featuring my travel photos from the last decade."

"That's extraordinary!"

"We won't be out of work, because you'll write the texts for the book. I already said that you agreed."

"I'm definitely on board!"

"On one condition," she says on a serious tone.

"Now I'm scared. What is it?"

"You're going to kick yourself in the butt and call Rahim. Am I being understood?"

"Yes, Mommy!"

Jean-Philippe misses his Hackney Wick neighborhood, populated by beatniks 2.0, their little eco-friendly and vegan cafés and their art workshops. In the early morning, he liked to run along the canal behind factories that displayed colorful graffiti painted by artists. Their protest works encouraged the hipsterization of the neighborhood. Jean-Philippe loves his bohemian life, feeling like the soul of an artist—a British version of 2010, complete with his checkered shirt.

The distance creates a void in him. He left Ithaca-on-the-Lake for Montreal to live in the frenzy of the metropolis.

Having relocated to London from Quebec for an entirely different reason, the memories in his childhood home serve as a constant reminder. He remains attached to his native town, but his life is organized elsewhere. In Ithaca-on-the-Lake, people don't live on the fringes of social rules, they follow them. Jean-Philippe was born there, and his roots runs deep in this rural village. He has now grown and spread his branches under the sun of the Old World. His leaves now sparkle under the blowing London wind.

Spread across two continents, how can he merge the past of Ithaca-on-the-Lake and the future of London? One foot in America and the other in Europe, an impossible gap to bridge. Where is the present? Should he deny the past or abandon his future?

On the radio, a song by Scorpions delivers a message to him. Naturally, he's familiar with "Wind of Change," although at times, there seems to be more wind than actual change.

As he walks into the living room, he observes a series of family photos on the wall: Felix in his football uniform and his nieces Camille and Charlie, whom he misses terribly. They were young when he left for London. He speaks to them on their birthdays and at Christmas, either by phone or Skype, telling them that Santa Claus has left them a present in London which he'll be sending by post. In one of the pictures, his mother is at the center, with him appearing tiny and disheveled.

Michelle kept in touch with her son. Every month, she would clandestinely call him to get updates, spending about twenty minutes relaying village gossip and family information. Jean-Philippe has sent his mother a postcard from every place he's visited, always selecting a card with captivating images to make her dream.

🌍 🌎 🌏

2007

"I put your postcards on the fridge using a magnet and replace them when I get a new one. Your father acts like it's nothing, but he spends a lot of time in front of the fridge. He thinks I don't notice, but I know he reads what you write to me."

"I hope you don't make him suffer too much!"

"He can take it! But you, when are you coming home?"

"I don't know if I'm ready. I work and travel a lot. You see it with the postcards."

"You should try to take a vacation at some point. Your nieces won't recognize you!"

"Are you concerned about the girls or yourself? This year, I'm planning to spend Christmas with friends. We'll go to the countryside north of London to relax."

"I understand. You're living your life, but don't forget about your family. You know how much I miss holding you in my arms, my dear Phil."

To: <u>amy.cromarty@worldcompass.com</u>

Hey Amy,

I have something you might like... If I say: bat and cave! LOL

I've decided to take us back to Slovenia. I loved this place so much, and since you got your revenge on me for all the fake bats, I thought you might enjoy revisiting Postojna.

Dig through your photo collection, or else you might need to make a return trip to Slovenia for new images. I know how much you adore caves…

You might be wondering why I picked this place. Well, it's not just because I miss you, although... I can't get those baby dragons we saw in the cave out of my mind. Their incredible ability to adapt to such a harsh environment with no light or food is remarkable.

I feel somewhat like those baby dragons; I don't know where I belong. I'm from Quebec, but I live in London. My heart is in England, yet my roots are in Quebec. Returning to Ithaca confuses me deeply. Do all expats experience the same conflicting emotions as I do?

We will have the chance to talk about it again,

J.P.

The Mythographers

FIRE AND WATER

By Jean-Philippe Genest
Photographs by Amy Cromarty

I have never been particularly drawn to fairy tales. I'm more of an *Indiana Jones* or *Pirates of the Caribbean* type. Despite everything, we can't help being moved by the architecture of the Renaissance and Medieval castles in which these famous stories generally take place: Versailles, Chambord, d'Ussé, or Neuschwanstein.

In Slovenia, in the small town of Postojna, southwest of Ljubljana, the capital, there are enormous caves inhabited by larger-than-life characters. Visualize, if you will, a vast throne room where dukes and duchesses, counts and countesses for a feast. Enter a gigantic hall carved out of the rocks, the illuminated walls offering an imperial yellow, even golden color, reminiscent of sumptuous legends.

The decor exudes magnificence infused with a touch of magic. Picture the thousands of natural ornaments and envision a lyrical tune sung by a choir resonating among stalactites and stalagmites ranging vastly in shape and size—some towering taller than cathedrals, while others undulate like limestone draperies. It's undeniably the perfect setting for a princess story.

Supernatural caves

As you enter the Postojna caves, the presence of small ponds scattered on the ground like mirrors adds to the sumptuousness of the scene, a majestic sight of the place owed solely to the resilience of water droplets. Indeed, the Postojna caves are hollowed out by hydrochemical erosion spanning a period of several million years. The underground rivers, more acidic than normal, dissolve the limestone, leaving room for cavities expanding over tens of meters.

Droplets seeping from the ceiling form thousands of stalactites. As it flows, the drop of water carries the limestone, leaving part of it before falling to the ground. The impact of the drop causes it to lose the limestone, which accumulates vertically, thus forming stalagmites. This accumulation takes place on an infinitesimal scale. For centuries, the caves have evolved hidden from view, creating natural environments completely separate from the outside world.

Whoever talks about medieval legends inevitably refers to fantastic animals that kings, queens, and knights rub shoulders with. Slovenia is no exception. Dragons, symbols of courage and power, have been seen in this country.

Moreover, according to Greek mythology, Jason and the Argonauts fought a dragon very close to Ljubljana in their quest to reach the Adriatic Sea. The Slovenian capital is also known as the City of Dragons.

An ecosystem of dragons

It was under the stamp of these legends that Slovenian villagers believed that the Postojna caves sheltered mysterious beasts. In the caves of the region, they discovered small animals measuring around fifteen centimeters, rather slender with translucent skin. They referred to these creatures as the offspring of dragons. Two four-toed legs at the front and two two-toed legs very far behind allow them to move; a thin fin along the body and two egret-shaped gills behind the head complete their anatomy. There was obviously no specialist to contradict the peasants. If they're not baby dragons, what are they?

This animal became mythical due to its unique character and therefore precious to the peasants who feared and respected it. The dragon evolved to be a symbol of Slovenian courage.

It wasn't until the late 19th century that scientists began to study the "baby dragons," which they formally identified as olms (*Proteus anguinus*), a species of urodele, referring to an amphibian that retains its tail as an adult, much like salamanders. The olm possesses remarkable adaptive traits. It is blind and capable of fasting for several years because of its habitat in complete darkness without access to food. The eel-like creature's adaptation to its habitat evokes parallels with Charles Darwin's theory of evolution. Postojna Cave showcases an ecosystem as unique and secluded as the Galapagos Islands, Darwin's favorite place.

On a short or long timescale, evolution leads to the emergence of new species, as individuals best suited to their environment tend to reproduce more, a concept tied to Darwin's theory of natural selection. Consequently, the olm demonstrates an impressive adaptation by being capable of living blind and fasting for up to a century.

Slovenian geography has joined the legend. Thanks to their unique appearance, salamanders are confused with dragons. A beast so rare and exceptional deserves to live in the most beautiful fairy tales and in a unique castle like Postojna. Personally, this strange creature will remain, in my creative mind, a real baby dragon.

Dragons and courage

Humans have this fabulous ability to adapt, so be your own dragon and make your cave the best for yourself. Embracing change requires courage. Indeed, I have a thought for immigrants, refugees, and displaced people who move willingly, by force, or out of spite. I wish them determination and resilience to confront adversities, to discover a place of peace and happiness.

The World Compass, August 2010

10.

THE CULT OF THE HERO

1990

Phileas Fogg faces a dilemma and Jean-Philippe wants to know what happens next.

> Aouda retired to a waiting-room, and there she waited, thinking of the simple and noble generosity, the tranquil courage of Phileas Fogg. He has sacrificed his fortune, and was now risking his life, all without hesitation, from duty, in silence.

Mr. Fogg puts his reputation and wealth on the line, yet he chooses to act like a hero. He gathers men to rescue the missing, among them Jean Passepartout, his traveling companion, despite the evident dangers. Life holds more value than mere chance. Through this story, Jean-Philippe acquires fundamental values that will remain with him throughout his life.

"The train had just been attacked by the Sioux and he decided to lead an expedition to save his friend. This is a crucial moment in the history. What do you think will happen?"

"It's hard to guess," exclaims Jean-Philippe. "He'll take a long time, but he has to help his friend. He can't just leave him!"

"Phileas Fogg has changed a lot, don't you think?"

"Yes. At first, he saw Passepartout only as his valet, but now he considers him a friend. At the beginning, Phileas Fogg was distant and everything seemed calculated, but now he's genuinely interested in the people he encounters, especially after meeting Mrs. Aouda."

"You're very insightful for your age, Phil. Do you think Mrs. Aouda feels the same?" his father inquires.

"I think she's in love with Phileas Fogg!" Jean-Philippe replies with great confidence.

"So do I. I believe this is when her feelings for him start to bloom, and she becomes aware of them."

"I think she admires his courage, and I believe they might eventually get married. After all, he was the one who saved her from the funeral pyre in India."

"We'll find out in the upcoming chapters. There aren't many pages left before we discover the outcome!" he exclaims, rising to his feet.

Marc places the book in its regular place and switches off the light, allowing his son to sleep.

Jean-Philippe finds himself unable to close his eyes. He gazes at the novel resting on the chest of drawers, his thoughts racing with the various potential outcomes and endings of the story. He can't wait any longer to know how the story unfolds.

Do you really think you will find your hero one day? You're not Mrs. Aouda! Who would want to come and save you in Ithaca?

He dismisses the negative thoughts from his saboteur. This time, he can't diminish his spirit. It's not unusual to feel affection for Phileas Fogg, even if he's a boy. With a smile, he places his hands behind his head and falls asleep.

March 2010

After the nurse departs from verifying all the tubes and taking Marc's blood pressure, Jean-Philippe puts the metal chair back in its original position. Michelle fills the blue plastic cup with water and passes it to Marc before sitting down to continue knitting. Michelle and Marc reminisce about their first meeting. Sometimes, Jean-Philippe feels like an intruder in their privacy, even if he knows these stories by heart. The long days in the hospital allow them to revisit the great moments of their lives, as if there is an emergency to take stock of them.

"Goodness, you were absolutely hilarious! You were walking around in those snug pants and that little striped shirt, looking like your head was larger than your shoulders!" Michelle says with laughter.

"I wasn't the worst. I didn't have the best score, but I did very well. You were just jealous," Marc teases.

"You're so wrong. Do you remember who beat you in the final that year? My team," she replies.

"By a few measly points!"

"Stop it, liar, it wasn't even close. It was a landslide victory."

"It's true that if I hadn't thrown my balls in the gutter, it would have been closer."

Michelle places her knitting needles on her knees and gazes at Marc with bright eyes. She has always admired his deadpan humor. Retrieving a piece of wool from her bag, she continues knitting.

"That's when I fell in love with you!" says Marc, looking at his wife.

"You said to me: You impress me, Miss Sullivan!" she replies.

He discreetly winks at Michelle, who smiles from her chair. Amid the challenging circumstances, Jean-Philippe relishes the ease of the conversation. Obviously, now is not the time to throw a wrench in the pond with his stories.

"So, it was Mom who was the heroine of that evening?" he asks.

"Your mother is a superwoman. She made many sacrifices to be with me," Marc says gently. "We worked hard to provide you and your brother with a good quality of life. Hockey and football were quite expensive."

"For Felix, I understand. I bought my bike with what I earned as a bag boy," Jean-Philippe remarks sarcastically.

Trying to respond, Marc chokes. Michelle gets up to help him, but he pushes her away delicately.

"It's okay," he says behind a groan. He takes a tissue to wipe his lips and spit out saliva. "Do you think we gave more to Felix than to you?"

"Yes, but looking back, I'm proud that I made the purchase on my own. I took better care of it."

"You almost slept with it!" replies his mother.

"I understand you," his father says. "Our parents weren't wealthy. I had to take something like a dozen jobs before landing at Canadair!"

"I handed over my paychecks to my parents to help with rent and groceries," says Michelle. "It was only in the three months leading up to our wedding that my mother returned my pay to put together my hope chest. We made the most of what little we had."

"When I was approached to join the city council, we had a long discussion to assess the pros and cons. There was a sense of pride in volunteering one's time, but it added more responsibility to your mother's already heavy load."

They'd opted for a higher quality of life by choosing to reside in Ithaca-on-the-Lake due to its peaceful environment, sense of community, and affordable housing prices.

For nearly two years, Marc served as a municipal councilor before stepping in at short notice to assume the role of mayor. His composed demeanor and analytic abilities were highly valued, leading to his subsequent election as mayor in the following elections. Concurrently, the village was experiencing rapid growth, prompting the council to propose establishing a full-time mayoral position with a reasonable salary, a proposition that the voters supported and accepted.

"I remember it vividly. I was around thirteen or fourteen years old back then. Felix was in college and after that at the police institute. You thought you'd have more time for your family, but it didn't turn out that way! When I was free after school, you were occupied with council duties in the evenings. As a result, I hardly saw you anymore, and I found that challenging."

"I wanted to work for your future and that of your brother, making Ithaca-on-the-Lake a village where it's pleasant to live."

"Actually, I felt like you were more invested in others than in our own family. It was my father whom I talked to in the evening before bedtime. He was the one offering me advice and teaching me things. I was your helper, as you said. During renovations, I held the Gyproc and you screwed it in. I brushed on the paint, and you rolled it. It wasn't the most enjoyable activity, but it allowed me to spend time with you. When you became mayor, I saw you less. Among my friends, it was like, 'Oh, the mayor's son...' but deep down, all I wanted was to have my old father back."

"I didn't know that. Why didn't you talk to me about it?"

"When could I have told you about it? You weren't there."

"Your father certainly made a significant impact in Ithaca. It's thriving now, with tourism and businesses flourishing."

"Don't get me wrong; this is me speaking as a teenager. At that time, I felt alone. I didn't have a brother or a father anymore. My mind was racing, trying to navigate through a whirlwind of changes in my body, and the person I relied on to guide me through life was occupied managing a town. But it's okay, it's all in the past now. I made it through my adolescence; I'm not dead. In fact, I'm doing quite well."

"I'm sorry for not being there for you more," says Marc. "I should have noticed. I relied too much on Michelle, and I should have taken on more responsibility myself."

It's the beginning of an apology. It's not what you expected, but it's a step in the right direction.

"You'll understand when you're in a relationship too!" Michelle remarks to her son.

"Exactly. I wanted to share that I have someone special in my life," says Jean-Philippe, gently clearing his throat.

"That's fantastic news!" exclaims his mother.

"Yes, we've been dating for two years now."

"Two years! Well, well! You didn't want to tell me! Were you hiding him?"

"Michelle, let him speak," Marc says calmly.

"I know you had trouble with my homosexuality," he says, turning to his mother. "I didn't want to burden you with that."

"You know I often say things I don't mean. We simply didn't know much about homosexuality, and we didn't discuss those subjects," she admits.

"What's his name?" asks his father.

"Rahim. His name is Rahim Strand."

Rahim resides in his thoughts, and the distance only accentuates the sense of absence. His love for Rahim grows stronger each day, yet he still resists surrendering himself to that love. When they sleep together, Jean-Philippe's hand naturally rests on Rahim's body. Rahim has become his world, and he can't fall asleep without sensing his presence close to him, reminiscent of when he was young and slept with his hand on his atlas. Rahim possesses an array of exceptional qualities: he's generous, gentle, understanding, and remarkably handsome. He appears magnificent, like the divinity Jean-Philippe had long awaited—a Greek god tailored just for him.

🌐 🌍 🌎

As Jean-Philippe makes his way to the hospital cafeteria on the first floor, he begins texting on his iPhone.
"Hello you."

You are so stupid. Why not "Hi, sexy" as usual? You're a real idiot.

He adjusts his phone, aiming it differently to ensure the message is sent effectively.
"Hey, Babe," Rahim responds simply.
Jean-Philippe's heart beats quickly with excitement.

You're ridiculous. Horny as a toad!

"Miss you."

You won't win a Pulitzer with this conversation! Did you press "Send"? It's long! Well, he's not answering. He's mad at you!

"Me too," Rahim writes.

Jean-Philippe receives the two most beautiful words of the week. He feels a lightness, a ton of bricks disappearing from his shoulders. He stretches his neck until he hears a crack and massages his stiffened muscles to relax them.

"Call you tomorrow."

"Okay, Babe."

He sends a heart emoji, prompting a smile from Jean-Philippe. Distance and time weigh heavily on his soul. He misses Rahim terribly and, right now, he closes his eyes and imagines his boyfriend close to him. He lays his head on Rahim's shoulder, mentally guiding his lover's hand to rest on his thigh. He imagines the warmth of Rahim's slender fingers and the tenderness of his soft skin.

Calm down, big boy! It's just a text. It means nothing!

Since returning to Quebec, Jean-Philippe has found himself undergoing an identity crisis reminiscent of a second adolescence, despite the lack of desire to revisit that particular era. Instead, he finds himself immersed in fragments of his past, observing a brewing conflict within his mind—a battle waged between the past and the future, between the present locale and distant realms, and between the yearning for freedom and the constraints that encumber him.

"Do you know the story of Bellerophon?" Jean-Philippe asks his father.

"No, it doesn't ring a bell. Michelle, have you ever heard about it?"

"That means nothing to me," she confirms.

"He's a man, a Greek hero."

"I enjoy it when you tell me stories. It's like reversing our roles. I read the adventures of Phileas Fogg to you, and now you're sharing the tales of a man whose name I can barely recall with us," his father remarks, laughing.

"Bellerophon. I'm sure you're more acquainted with the secondary characters in the myth than the hero. Are you familiar with Pegasus? And the Chimera?

"Yes, the horse with wings!" exclaims his mother.

"That's Pegasus. However, Bellerophon is undoubtedly one of my favorite characters. Everyone knows about Achilles, the one with the heel, and Ulysses, the mastermind behind the Trojan horse. Bellerophon, on the other hand, is far less recognized."

Rising from his seat, Jean-Philippe eagerly acts out the scenes of the story. A natural-born storyteller, he believes in the power of legends to communicate messages that are often challenging to express otherwise.

"You should know that Bellerophon is the son of Eurynome and Glaucus, the king of Corinth. It's believed that his mother's lineage carries divine heritage, as she's the daughter of Sisyphus. What's crucial to understand is that Bellerophon is born of noble birth, a prince blessed with the gift of beauty and virility. A bit like Rahim. I'll show you some pictures," he adds.

"Yes, I want to see him," his mother says playfully.

"Let him finish his story," insists his father.

"In essence, during a discus-throwing session with his brother, Bellerophon unintentionally kills him—an unfortunate accident. Nevertheless, following the Ancient Greek tradition, he's compelled to go into exile to atone for his crime and seeks refuge with King Proteus. Naturally, he's received with honor and, due to his remarkable appearance, the queen attempts to seduce him."

"Oh, what a naughty girl!"

"But Bellerophon declines her advances. He knows how to maintain proper conduct. However, feeling frustrated by this rejection, the queen informs her husband that Bellerophon has made advances toward her and that she finds it to be inappropriate. Obviously, the enraged king seeks Bellerophon's demise, although the law of that era prohibits the putting to death of a guest. So, the king devises a plan and sends Bellerophon with a sealed letter to his father-in-law, King Iobates. The letter contains a request for Bellerophon's assassination, along with the reasons why he has to do it."

"That's worse than my afternoon soap operas!" says Michelle.

"King Iobates is very happy to host a prince of Bellerophon's caliber and welcomes him with open arms. It isn't until several days later that the king finally reads the letter detailing Bellerophon's wrongdoing. So, King Iobates finds himself in a dilemma—he has already offered shelter to Bellerophon, making him unable to execute the order outlined in the letter."

Jean-Philippe pauses in his story. He calculates its effect. His father appears captivated, while his mother shifts in her seat. He loves this feeling.

"So, Iobates gets an idea. He assigns Bellerophon the task of defeating the indomitable Chimera, a creature that has been wreaking havoc in his kingdom. Aware that no one could possibly succeed, Bellerophon would die, thus ending the story. Ultimately, they'd be rid of the problem."

"Obviously, it won't end like that," said Michelle.

"You're quite right. The young man can't refuse, so he embarks on a quest to hunt down the monster—an entity with the body of a goat, the head of a lion, and the tail of a snake. At first, he spies on the Chimera, noting its great speed and its ability to breathe fire like a dragon. During the night, he receives a visit from the goddess Athena. You do remember that Bellerophon has a connection with the gods of Olympus? The Goddess of Wisdom enlightens him about Pegasus, revealing the possibility of taming the winged horse. Only a flying horse can be swift enough to evade the Chimera's flames. Riding Pegasus, he soars above the Chimera and slays the creature."

"It does end well," says Michelle.

"Officially, the story doesn't end well. It's not a Hollywood movie. Bellerophon's excessive pride becomes arrogance. First, he seeks revenge on the queen who falsely accused him by taking her for a ride on the back of Pegasus, then pushes her into the sea from the skies. Later, believing himself worthy of a place among the gods, he sets out to fly to Olympus on the back of his winged stallion. Incensed by this insolence, Zeus, the king of the gods, reacts in anger, sending a gadfly to sting Pegasus. Bellerophon tumbles from the sky and is left crippled and blinded by the fall. From that moment on, he wanders the earth until his eventual death."

"Wow! Quite an ending. I liked it better when it ended with the death of the Chimera," says Marc.

"In every story, whatever they may be, there are multiple lessons to be learned. Myths often serve as a reflection of our societies or our shortcomings. Each aspect of the legend can touch us and resonate differently with individuals. In myths, interpretation plays a pivotal role.”

“I see a certain resilience there, when he faces several betrayals,” says Michelle. “In the end, the truth triumphed despite everything.”

“I see that it's okay to get help. He receives help from Athena to achieve his goals,” says Marc.

“You have interesting interpretations. I find myself torn between the symbolism of Pegasus, representing freedom, and the Chimera, symbolizing the objective to be achieved—the monster to be slain,” Jean-Philippe says with a smile that conceals a half-truth.

There’s no doubt about Jean-Philippe's clarity of mind. He understands precisely why he dreams of these two mythical beings. Pegasus embodies true freedom, serving as the vehicle propelling him toward his ambitions. Through encounters in both internal exploration and external realms, he discovers himself. Isn't that the essence of it all?

However, the Chimera exists as a creation of the imagination, an illusion dwelling deep within his unconscious. It consumes his energy and obstructs his ride on Pegasus. Contrary to his belief, the Chimera isn’t his father; rather, it lives within him as a saboteur and an imposter. Jean-Philippe now faces the ultimate battle: the fight against himself, the struggle for his very existence.

11.

A SMOKE SCREEN

August 2008

Along with their circle of friends, Jean-Philippe and Amy come together to celebrate the publication of Amy's photographs in *Playboy* magazine. They don't ask for as much to organize a celebration and have a pint of beer or two. For Amy, it's not an accomplishment, but the situation is amusing enough to throw a party.

Explaining the presence of landscape photos in an erotic magazine, she says, "It allows men to justify to their girlfriends that they read the magazine for the articles!"

Jean-Philippe and Amy's friends have gathered at the Admiral Duncan, a quaint pub nestled in the Soho district, with the capacity for no more than a hundred customers. The pub's elegant, sapphire-blue exterior, adorned with rainbow flags, stands proudly in the vibrant heart of the gay district. Bistro tables now sprawl across Old Compton Street, transformed into a pedestrian zone for a few weeks during the summer.

The bar boasts an extensive counter lined with a tantalizing array of alcohol bottles that could make any customer's mouth water. Samuel and Andrew, a couple whom Jean-Philippe encountered shortly after arriving in London, await them inside the pub. During their initial meeting, they extended an invitation to Jean-Philippe for a night of threesome sex at their apartment. Following a few hours of conversation, flirtation, and numerous pints of beer, Jean-Philippe eventually agreed. However, their dynamic evolved into a purely platonic friendship, despite the enjoyable encounter. Sam, a real estate broker, found accommodations for him in the Hackney district, while Andy became his gym companion.

"You missed the colossus this week," Andy confides to him. "I'm certain you would've been infatuated. You and bodybuilders!"

"It always happens when I'm not there," says Jean-Philippe. "There's still the dashing Connor, casually pumping his pectorals in front of the mirror as if no one were watching him."

"Don't waste your time; he's straight."

"Perhaps he could succumb to my charm!"

"With your thighs of steel," Andy says, laughing.

"I could drop a weight and show him my butt," he says, leaning over.

"Has it ever worked?"

The discussion continues in a bawdy manner, growing more animated, free-spirited, and untroubled. A sense of complete freedom reigns among the gathering crowds within the cozy confines of the pub.

"Don't start talking about sex without me!" Amy interrupts, joining the conversation amid the males in heat. "Save some for me! I'm missing out."

"We tried to match you with a couple guys, but you're missing a few pieces," Sam says, pointing to his crotch.

"I have more balls than you, my crazy bunch," she quips.

"It's true! You're more masculine than many of us!" Jean-Philippe laughs.

Since collaborating with Jean-Philippe, Amy has discovered an unknown world: the gay bars, a realm less formal and pretentious than traditional bars. In these spaces, she allows herself to enjoy the evening without the perpetual unease of flirtation and the false games of seduction, fully aware that these venues aren't where she anticipates finding her life partner.

"You can be our fag hag," Andy told him.

"Ugh! That's an ugly word... Why not say I'll be your fairy godmother?" She laughs, lifting her arm with a touch of elegance.

"Your Majesty!" He bows.

Amy is having a blast, belting out rock hits from the late 20th century blasting through the speakers. Gemma, her sister, and Gemma's husband, Stuart, join the group as Amy delves into her second pint of beer. As the evening reaches its peak, about ten friends from diverse backgrounds gather together. Conversations are loud to overcome the music.

Jean-Philippe leans in to listen to Stuart, who is attempting to convert him into a football fan while advocating for the colors of Manchester United. The Cromarty sisters sway to the rhythm of Madonna's beats, spilling some beer around them. Meanwhile, Andy holds Sam close, planting kisses on his neck. Observing them, Jean-Philippe feels a tinge of jealousy toward their relationship, which has endured for more than a decade. The previous summer, Amy accompanied Jean-Philippe to the couple's ceremony commemorating their ten years together. They exchanged vows under a pavilion in the English countryside, a beautiful and romantic moment.

Two drag queens come forward to introduce the karaoke evening. After cracking a few daring jokes, one of them, clothed in her sequined dress, a vibrant multi-colored boa, and her oversized wig, invites Amy and Jean-Philippe onto the stage for the next song. Amy signed them up for the performance without her best friend's knowledge. He finishes the last of his pint of Guinness before joining Amy on the small stage, illuminated by colorful spotlights.

"Before we kick things off, let me share some exciting news: Amy, here, recently had photos featured in *Playboy* magazine!" Jean-Philippe announces amid cheers from the crowd. "But let me clarify, it's not about seeing her naked in the magazine—no one here's looking for that! Instead, I raise my glass—sorry, my microphone—to celebrate your success, my friend."

The exuberant patrons chuckle and raise their glasses in a toast to Amy's achievement as the notes of a U2 song start playing.

Jean-Philippe and Amy lock eyes as they sing this song with the intensity of a Greek tragedy, amplifying their arm movements to impart a deeper significance, giving a broader meaning than the lyrics suggest. Fueled by alcohol, the intensity of their gestures compensates for any lack of accuracy in their signing. Their friends at the table shout words of encouragement, infusing Jean-Philippe and Amy with the enthusiasm to amplify their vocal performance even further. When the title of the song "I Still Haven't Found What I'm Looking For" appears on the screen, everybody in the pub joins in the singing with Jean-Philippe and Amy.

From the stage, Jean-Philippe casts a glance at the crowd before him and notices a strikingly handsome man at the bar. Suddenly, his surroundings seem to dim and blur, leaving only the man's face in sharp focus, as if a spotlight were illuminating him alone. Despite his hazy mind, Jean-Philippe delivers his lines like a seasoned theater actor, his attention fixed on this captivating figure. With alluring gestures, he attempts to captivate this beautiful Adonis with his performance.

The handsome man gazes at him, offering a slight smile that accentuates his perfect teeth. His Mediterranean complexion complements his lustrous, jet-black hair elegantly styled to the side. Jean-Philippe imagines running his hand though the man's hair and sliding it along his cheek. At the end of the verse, he extents his arm toward this captivating beauty, conveying that he's singing for him, solely for him. At his side, Amy screams, bending over slightly, channeling the strength of her diaphragm to finish the song.

The crowd cheers the singers on, marking a moment of connection between the handsome man and Jean-Philippe. For a fraction of a second, their eyes meet, and Jean-Philipp's heart skips a beat. Will the hook of seduction bear fruit on this evening of rejoicing? Is that stranger the one he's looking for?

Before starting to repeat the chorus, Jean-Philippe sees the Apollo-like figure moving away from the bar, making his way toward the exit. Under the influence of alcohol, he cries out his disappointment with, "Fuck you, man!" creating an outburst in the audience, as if it gives new meaning to the lyrics. Frantically finishing the song, Jean-Philippe places an arm on Amy's shoulders, promising to pay for the next round. The crowd applauds as they walk off the stage, arms raised in victory.

Jean-Philippe orders two pints of Guinness at the bar and carries them over to Amy. Afterward, he politely excuses himself for some fresh air. Sam and Andy join him briefly before quietly departing. They exchange kisses on the cheeks, promising to meet later in the week for the gym, dinner, or to chat in a quieter environment. Smiling, Andy and Sam walk away hand in hand.

Outside on the impromptu terrace facing the Admiral Duncan, a gentle, refreshing breeze offers Jean-Philippe a moment of relief, his forehead damp with sweat. He puts down his glass to adjust his hair, fixing some strands that had come loose from his bun. As he turns around, he notices the attractive man smoking a cigarette a few meters away, the same individual he was glancing at during his performance of the U2 song. He turns his head, stealing glimpses out the corner of his eye, alternating his gaze between the asphalt and the magnificent male standing there.

Normally clumsy in such situations, Jean-Philippe gathers his courage and casually strolls toward the Greek god-like man in a suit. He has always preferred to express his interest by dancing provocatively on a dance floor, which would be rather inappropriate in the middle of the street. He approaches timidly, trying to establish eye contact, but the guy remains absorbed in his phone. Moving closer, he patiently waits for him to finish his cigarette before carefully placing his glass of beer on his bistro table.

"Excuse me, would you mind?" he asks politely.

"Of course!" the man replies, offering a small, embarrassed yet courteous smile.

Jean-Philippe discerns a splendid British accent with impeccable diction. It's an obvious extrapolation, as detecting perfect pronunciation after just two words seems improbable. The gentleman wears a navy blue suit and a finely lined shirt.

Pretty chic, he thinks, noticing the undone collar button. He can't help but imagine nuzzling into the curve of the man's neck.

"My name is Jean-Philippe," he says, using an English accent to disguise his French-speaking first name.

"Nice to meet you. I'm Rahim. You're French?" he asks.

"French from Canada."

French from Canada, really?

"It's still the Commonwealth."

"Yes, but don't mention that to my compatriots from Quebec!"

"True, I do know a bit about the geopolitical situation in Canada. Care for a cigarette?"

"With pleasure."

Jean-Philippe holds the cigarette between his fingers, using it as a distraction while continuing to talk, attempting to steer the conversation away from the previous topic.

"You're quite elegant for a karaoke evening like tonight," he continues.

"I went to grab dinner with colleagues after work, and I didn't feel like heading straight home. The night is beautiful, and I wanted to make the most of it."

"That makes sense!" he says awkwardly. "After the song, I had to step out. It was pretty hot under the spotlights."

"I noticed. You did great, and it's true, it gets stuffy in there. It's small, but I adore this place."

Stop talking about the temperature. It's a bit conventional as a subject and not very original. Look at you, you're sweating way too much. You're not at the top of your game. You should go back inside.

Rahim approaches Jean-Philippe to light the cigarette.

"No, thank you, I don't smoke!"

Rahim steps back with a puzzled look and lights his cigarette.

"I never turn down a gift," he says proudly. "No matter how small. At the very least, it'll be a souvenir of our meeting," he adds in a somewhat cheesy tone.

Did you really just say that? You're really bad. No need to sabotage you; you do it all by yourself... Ask him if it's going to rain tomorrow while you're at it.

He bites the inside of his cheek, but Rahim continues the conversation without seeming to notice any discomfort in Jean-Philippe, who manages to maintain his smile.

"I'd like to quit, but it's difficult. It's mostly a habit because I don't particularly enjoy cigarettes. I began to manage stress with them. I haven't found, as they say, the motivation to stop!"

"There are various ways to discover motivation," Jean-Philippe expresses, taking on a quasi-life coach role.

He takes Rahim's cigarette and throws it on the ground, crushing it. Then he returns his to the packet, which he places back in his jacket pocket.

"I can leave you my phone number. If you don't have anyone... Well, I mean, if you're free and single, obviously."

"Yes, I'm single. And I'd be happy to continue the conversation," Rahim replies with a smile.

He lends him his iPhone so that Jean-Philippe can enter his number.

"When you feel the urge to smoke, just give me a call, and I'll help you find that motivation. I'm quite adept at motivating people, and I'd love to motivate you."

"I always feel like smoking before I go to sleep."

"Perfect! I'm full of motivation at that time!"

They continue to converse for a few minutes before Jean-Philippe excuses himself to rejoin Amy and their friends inside. Honestly, whether Rahim smokes or not doesn't bother him; he simply wanted to find a reason for Rahim to call him back.

The very next day, he and Rahim meet in an Asian restaurant. They share a meal of sushi, delving into discussions about their professions, goals, and aspirations. Jean-Philippe discovers that Rahim works in a bank and has two younger sisters. Rahim's mother originates from Mumbai, which explains his dark complexion; she works for a hospital foundation, while his British father manages a business. An avid cricket fan, he has been playing the sport since adolescence. Although Jean-Philippe doesn't share much about his family, he talks about the expeditions he has undertaken for work and the stories that have led him abroad. Rahim, on the other hand, reveals that he has visited India twice to see his mother's family, marking the extent of the travels in his young life.

Rahim quit smoking, and they had maintained an almost daily conversation for two years. Since Jean-Philippe's arrival in Quebec, he hasn't spoken to Rahim, marking the longest period of silence since they first met. This weighs heavily on Jean-Philippe's mind, and he feels the urgency to rectify it as soon as possible.

Are you rebuilding the bridge with your father while damaging the one with your handsome Apollo?

12.

THE DIVINE TREMORS

2010

The whole family waits in silence for the meeting with Doctor Gauthier. Michelle sits close to Marc, Felix nervously bites his nails on the metal chair, and Jean-Philippe leans against the wall. Heavy rain drums on the window, punctuating the gloom in the eighth-floor bedroom.

As the doctor enters, she begins discussing the recent tests analyses—rambling about figures and results. However, Marc abruptly interrupts her speech.

"How long, Doctor?" he asks.

"Hmm, it's difficult to predict. It can deteriorate quickly, or it might last up to three months. With prompt treatment, it could extend to six months, and possibly longer if you respond well."

Marc looks at his wife for a moment, smiling at her.

"Thank you, Doctor, but I've made my decision."

In a firm and assertive manner, he states, "I won't undergo any treatments. No chemo, no procedures on my body."

"But… Dad!" Felix exclaims, rising from his chair.

Jean-Philippe, also taken aback, straightens up, his gaze shifting between his father and mother.

"Listen, Mr. Genest. I'll be returning tomorrow anyway. We can then address any other questions you might have. Don't rush your decision. Take tonight to think about it. Have a discussion as a family, and we'll revisit the topic tomorrow. I'll honor your decision, but I strongly advise you to consider it carefully. All right?"

The doctor departs, leaving Jean-Philippe pacing in the confined space near the room's entrance. Felix resumes his seat, while Michelle tightly holds Marc's hand, tears streaming down her cheeks.

"Is your decision final?" asks Michelle.

"Yes, I've been thinking about it for several days. The doctor can conduct all the analyses she wants, but I won't proceed any further. I refuse to undergo treatments that can make me sicker to gain two more months."

"We can't be certain. You might respond well to the treatments and potentially gain a few more years," Jean-Philippe suggests.

"Look who's talking. He disappears for years and then suddenly decides on what his father has to do!" Felix retorts, glaring at his brother. "You have some nerve!"

"Felix, calm down!" Marc admonishes him.

"Yes, yes, it's okay. Sorry."

Felix stands up and takes a deep, audible breath. With their arms crossed, the two brothers form a barricade near the bed, Felix's imposing stature contrasting with that of Jean-Philippe.

"You're not even willing to consider the treatments? I assumed you'd want to fight. You've just turned sixty-three. It's too young," argues Jean-Philippe. "You have two granddaughters. Don't you want to see them grow up?"

"My body can't endure it any longer. If you felt a fraction of the pain I feel, you'd understand. I wouldn't wish it on anyone."

In silence, Michelle wipes her cheeks with the back of her hand. Jean-Philippe exits the room, pacing the corridor. His face is flushed, heat flooding his forehead—not a fever, but a volcano of emotions, an eruption of incomprehension. He hasn't come all this way, returning to his origins, only to witness his father's passing.

It's an avoidance, a lack of courage. Could this be selfishness? After all, Jean-Philippe is well aware of all the symptoms.

At the end of the corridor, he gazes out at the vast suburbs encircling the hospital grounds, his attention wandering to the horizon. Jean-Philippe reflects on his own departure, his journey to Europe. Why do people flee? To evade pain, because it feels unbearable, insurmountable. Yet when suffering catches up, we must confront it and battle against it. Why doesn't his father choose to fight? Despite his own fear, Jean-Philippe chose to return to Quebec to face his pain. Over the past few days, he has sensed progress, feeling as if he's making strides, that he's able to better communicate with his father. Each small step he takes reinforces him to move forward, despite the immense energy it demands.

He chooses to confront his fears because he believes he stands a chance of overcoming them. Jean-Philippe can win this battle. However, his father... Two months, four months, six months… Ultimately, the result remains unchanged. He must reassess his own decisions and, in this instance, acknowledge that the struggles prompting him to flee are incomparable to the depth of Marc's suffering.

As he re-enters the room, a silence hangs in the air. Jean-Philippe is certain that Marc won't reconsider his decision. He knows his father's stubbornness; the apple doesn't fall far from the tree. Marc's choice remains his sole grasp on control. He takes his position by the bedside, facing his father and mother, who remain seated, holding onto Marc's hand.

"Did you know that, around the world, the origin of earthquakes is different from one place to another?" asks Jean-Philippe.

"What are you talking about?" Felix exclaims, grumbling in his chair.

"The earthquakes, the ground moving, the buildings collapsing," he replies with a touch of sarcasm.

"I know what an earthquake is. I'm not stupid."

"So, let me continue," Jean-Philippe says, pausing to catch his breath. "While researching myths, I was surprised to discover that, across various regions, the explanations for earthquakes are diverse and, at times, more imaginative than others."

"Like what? Give me an example," asks Marc, happy to change the atmosphere of the room.

"In the north of Russia, in Siberia, a land of snow and cold, it's said that the earth rests on a sleigh led by the god Tuli and that it's pulled by dogs that have fleas. When the ground starts to shake, it's said that it's the dogs who have stopped to scratch themselves."

"That's strange," comments Michelle.

"Here's another: In New Zealand, the population associates earthquakes with Mother Earth, who carries the god Ruaumoko in her womb. When he stretches and kicks, he causes earthquakes."

"That's ridiculous!" protests Felix.

"I think that explanation makes a lot of sense," his mother intervenes. "If you'd experienced carrying a child, you might understand better."

"I must admit, it would be quite amusing to see you pregnant, Felix," Jean-Philippe remarks.

"Shut up, it's not funny!"

"In Greece, the philosopher Aristotle said it was the winds that were locked in caves which, struggling to escape, shook the country."

"As if we could catch the wind. Sure!"

"Stop taking this at face value, Felix. They're legends, stories to give meaning to what we don't always understand," he says, exasperated. "The Greeks even saw the positive in certain disasters. Poseidon, a god with a feisty temperament, threw monster tantrums, which caused earthquakes. As much as it's attributed with destruction and floods, it's also credited with the gushing of hot water springs which can cure many illnesses."

"Where are you going with these stories?" Felix asks.

"I understand," Marc expresses, looking Jean-Philippe in the eyes.

The room falls into silence again while waiting for the rest of the response.

"My decision may not make sense to you, but it makes sense to me. I could try to explain it at length, but I wouldn't be able to express it properly. Like an earthquake, illness can knock you off your feet. We ask ourselves: why me? What did I do? We fall apart, we pick up the pieces, but we have to make do. It's difficult to explain and accept, but I ask you to respect my decision."

In his best way of being pragmatic, Jean-Philippe resumes his thoughts. "Today, science has advanced significantly. Seismographs can precisely locate the origin of earthquakes and predict underground activities, even the slightest tremors, owing to advanced technology. However, predicting outcomes for the human body is complex. Therefore, yes, I will respect your decision. I may not be pleased with it, but I'll respect it."

13.

HEADWINDS

"Hello, sexy!"

"Hello, Babe! How are you?"

"It could be better, but it's okay. Am I bothering you?"

"No. I'm watching a match on TV."

"Cricket? Which teams?"

"Australia versus New Zealand! Go Black Caps!" Rahim shouts.

Jean-Philippe chuckles at the sound of his screams. He has very little interest in televised sports, except for admiring the attractive players, particularly in American football where the snug pants highlight their physique. Another sport that captivates Jean-Philippe is Olympic diving. His enthusiasm for this sport is evident. During cricket matches with Rahim, Jean-

Philippe often dozes off on Rahim's shoulder or delves into a book, comfortably sprawled across him. Rahim takes the opportunity to hold him close, caressing his hair or massaging his legs and feet. Suddenly, Jean-Philippe finds himself more inclined to watch cricket alongside Rahim.

"How's your father doing?"

"It's challenging. He's on painkillers and sleeps a lot. The cancer has spread, so the doctor opted not to proceed with a more invasive operation. Chemotherapy was offered, but he declined. While it might have prolonged his life by a few weeks or months, it wouldn't have altered the inevitable outcome. According to his doctor, he doesn't have much time left. He chose quality of life and is at peace with his decision. As for me, I spend most of my days with him."

"And your mother? How does she take this?"

"It's painful for her too, but she doesn't display it openly. I believe she's trying to stay strong for my dad and for the family. I don't think she fully comprehends the severity of my father's illness yet."

"And you, are you holding up?"

"I'm trying, obviously. I find it difficult to see my father in this condition. He has become frail and has lost a significant amount of weight. Despite everything, there are days when he's in better spirits. He enjoys it when I share travel stories and anecdotes with him. That's how we pass the time together."

"You won't miss it, especially with Amy!" Rahim mocks.

"I'm doing my best to keep him entertained. By the way, could you go to the apartment and send me some files? You can scan them or email them to me. I plan to stay here a bit longer. I've spoken to my editor, and I'll be working remotely from here. At the moment, I won't be taking on any assignments and will only concentrate on The Mythographers with articles I've already written."

"Of course, I'll do that. You tell me which ones; otherwise there's no way I can digitize everything!"

"I know!"

"At worst, I'll ask Amy. Do you need anything else?"

"No, it's fine, I can manage. I left in a rush, and I didn't bring all my clothes, so I've been washing a lot! I'll buy some new ones when I find a little free time," Jean-Philippe says.

Tears stream down his cheeks, and his voice is choked with sobs. A silence settles.

"I'm here, Babe," Rahim reassures him.

"I'm so tired, Rahim. Utterly exhausted. I wake up in the morning feeling as if I haven't slept at all. I have no energy left. My thoughts are swirling. I feel so confused. There are so many things I want to express to my father, but the words won't come out! I'm just like him! I wish we could take the time to genuinely talk, to halt the innuendoes. It's tearing me apart inside."

"I'm sure he appreciates it just that you're there."

"I want him to know that I'm not a failure, that I've worked hard to reach where I am. You're aware of everything I contribute to the magazine. I'm not the 'big doofus' of five years ago. I don't want to be a disappointment to my father anymore. Not now. Not ever again."

"I know. You have to give him time."

"But we're running out of time! He has truly accepted his fate and keeps moving forward. I'm trailing behind like a small dog, attempting to catch up and to slow him down. Damn! I feel so inadequate beside him, as if I don't measure up. But how do I make him see who I've become? Am I putting too much pressure on myself? Why do I still seek validation from my father? I know I'm a competent journalist. I'm a damn good reporter! All I want is for him to acknowledge it. I want him to be proud of me. That's all."

The sobbing resumes. The phone adheres to his damp cheek and Jean-Philippe clings to the device as if seeking warmth from his lover. In that precise moment, he yearns to seek refuge in Rahim's arms, to find solace and remain there indefinitely. He just wants to lay his head on Rahim's shoulder, letting go of thoughts, decisions, and the ceaseless whirlwind in his mind.

"I love you, Babe."

"I love you too, Rahim. I was so scared that it was the end of us. I didn't hear from you, and I thought you wouldn't want to continue with a coward like me, after everything I said."

"Listen to me. When I made the decision to be with you, it wasn't a whim. I was committed to our relationship. Your heart is as vast as the earth itself. You embrace me for who I am, and your smile illuminates every room. You're also the bravest person I've ever known. You travel to war-torn countries, sleep in the most unclean places. I couldn't handle that. You underestimate yourself, JP. I'm not sure I could confront my mother as you're doing with your father."

"I sent you so much nonsense."

"You weren't yourself. I know you. I simply wanted to give you space and time because I thought that's what you needed. That's all. But I'm here, and I'm not going anywhere. You're stuck with me."

Jean-Philippe receives Rahim's touching words like a balm on his insecurities. So many moments where he advances with his head down, reclusive, withdrawn into himself.

"Courageous" is definitely not the word I would use to describe you. Does Rahim have a good perception of you?

"Ah! Shut up!" shouts Jean-Philippe, in his well-known Quebecer accent.

"Sorry, what? I didn't understand," says Rahim.

"I was talking to myself. It wasn't aimed at you."

"I can't wait to see you! Watching cricket without you isn't the same," he says.

"Really? Either I fall asleep, or I read while you listen to the matches."

"It keeps my hands busy. I massage your legs before undoing your pants and making love to the most beautiful man on Earth."

"I miss you so much," declares Jean-Philippe. "Of course, I wouldn't mind some sex with you, right now."

"I can't wait to kiss you again and spoon with you, smell your hair and hold your hand and cross our fingers on your chest."

"I want to feel your body against mine."

"You know that you can come and live with me. I already offered it to you," Rahim insists.

"I know that, but now isn't the right time to bring up that subject. You know I'm always a mess. When you visit me, you align the containers on the counter. You put my dishes in the cupboards. You take care of watering my plants. Your condo isn't a place for two. I enjoy our weekends together, but

I'm careful not to leave anything lying around. You're the one who ensures my toothbrush goes back in the jar because I tend to leave it on the edge of the sink. I'm going to feel out of place. I'm not as orderly as you are. Everything is very tidy. I rinse my mouth, taking the water with my hands so as not to dirty the glass in the bathroom. We're so different. I'm going to get on your nerves."

"We've been together for two years now, and I understand your habits quite well. If it bothered me that you don't put the cap back on the toothpaste tube, I would have mentioned it. I want us to live together and build our future together."

"I know what I'm like! I don't want you to regret your decision, and I'm not prepared to experience any more disappointments. Not now."

"We'll have to make a choice at some point. I want to live with my lover."

"I know that, but right now, I don't have time to think about that. I know I disappoint you when I speak like this. I'm sorry."

"I'm not telling you to rush your decision. I've given you time and space. What I truly desire is for us to share the same space, all the time. You know how I am. I need to be organized, to know where we're going. Don't get me wrong; I don't want to control you. I have complete trust in you, but I need to predict my next steps, to control where I'm going. Having two apartments complicates things—yours, mine. I simply wish it could be straightforward. That's all," Rahim expresses kindly.

"I know all that. You have a clearer vision than me. Rahim, when I become overly structured, I tend to feel overwhelmed. I want it to be easy too. For now, simplicity is the status quo. I can't live with changes. When things move too much, I feel dizzy."

"I'll be there to catch you if you fall."

"Sometimes I need to improvise. Are you ready for that?"

Here's the exit! Come on, run away. Run away.

To: <u>amy.cromarty@worldcompass.com</u>

Dear Amy,

I think you'll be happy to know that I spoke with Rahim, and we set the record straight. I love him so much, it can't be explained. Knowing you both are far from me is painful, as if a part of me hasn't made the trip to Quebec. At least I know that you have my well-being at heart, and I'll make sure to stay strong to come back healthy! Was it convincing? LOL

In the text I'm sending you, I revisit our trip to Thailand. Maybe it's love or simply that I think I feel like a snake shedding its old skin. One thing's for sure, reconnecting with my roots has contributed to my personal evolution. Initially, I left with a singular purpose in mind, but today, it seems less significant.

Do I seem to be calming down? NEVER! LOL… We always have a blast together. That keeps me far from becoming dull.

See you soon, my crazy girlfriend!

J.P.

The Mythographers

THE SNAKE CHARMER

By Jean-Philippe Genest
Photographs by Amy Cromarty

In the mythology of the Kingdom of Siam, now known as Thailand, Nagas hold significance as important symbols of the country, alongside the elephant and the cassava flower. Nagas are mythical serpents of Hinduism that are present in various facets of the country's culture, traditions, and arts.

Legend has it that the Mekong River, flowing through Indochina, was shaped by a colossal snake slithering through the land and carving the bed of the expansive waterway. Revered by Buddhists as the protector of waters and natural treasures, this snake embodies an important symbol of prosperity and enduring longevity, notably attributed to its annual shedding of skin.

Naka Cave, situated at the heart of Phu Langka National Park, boasts walls that bear a texture reminiscent of snake scales. Local inhabitants have engaged in extensive debates regarding the rock's origin, speculating whether it might be a giant petrified reptile or even a fossil.

The Legend of Prince Fahoong

Centuries ago, a prince named Fahoong resided within the Rappata Nakhon Kingdom. Towering, strong, and blessed with good looks, he stood as the kingdom's most prominent bachelor and cherished friend to all. However, despite his wealth, a lingering sense of solitude thwarted his quest for true love.

One day, while strolling through the forest, the prince heard a young woman singing. He was captivated by the sweet yet wistful melody, and it stirred a deep affection within him. Despite his efforts to locate her, she remained unseen. As he turned back, he heard the cries of the same young woman resonating in his heart. While searching in the woods, the prince discovered only a shed snakeskin, which he took along with him.

The young girl was named Nakkarintrani, and her tears conveyed the injustice of her people's law. She witnessed a handsome man with the most radiant smile, yet she would never have the chance to meet him. Her predicament stemmed from a secret she harbored—she was a Nagi. The Nagas (with "Nagi" as the female form) were semi-divine serpents capable of transforming into human shape. Moreover, Nakkarintrani, the eldest daughter of the great lord of the Nagas entrusted with safeguarding Earth's riches, was bound by strict laws prohibiting marriage to a human.

Determined to find the prince, Nakkarintrani revisited the forest several times, and one sunny day, fate brought them together. Their love blossomed instantly. Over the following weeks, Fahoong's word and deeds radiated immense kindness, prompting the Nagi to confide her secret in him. As they shared a kiss, the prince proposed to her, and without hesitation, she accepted his heartfelt proposal.

At the Royal Palace, Prince Fahoong awaited the king's decision. The king had summoned Lord Naka to discuss a possible arrangement. Both parties granted their blessing, but on one condition: no one should know his daughter's secret. Otherwise, they would face banishment from the kingdom. Furthermore, if the secret were discovered, the entire kingdom would suffer from Lord Naka's fury.

Prince Fahoong paid little attention to this as he was blissful. He had married the most beautiful woman on Earth. However, she faced the challenge of being unable to conceive children, and after several years, the populace criticized her for not producing heirs for the kingdom. Despite enduring the insults, she withdrew into her chambers, even refusing to eat. Gradually, she lost her vitality, and maintaining her human appearance became increasingly difficult. To recuperate, she sought solace into her animal form.

One morning, the maid entered the room and found a huge snake lying in the princess's bed. "Don't be afraid, I am Nakkarintrani," she hissed. The servant panicked and rushed to alert the palace, shouting that the princess had transformed into a snake. The news quickly reached Lord Naka's ears, leading him to accuse the king and the prince of betraying their promise.

That night, the lord arrived at the kingdom accompanied by his soldiers—twenty-foot-long snakes with venomous fangs. Within hours, the kingdom lay in ruins, the city reduced to ashes, and no inhabitants remained alive. However, Fahoong and Nakkarintrani were never discovered. Some speculate that they fled into a small cave, destined to endure pain and hunger, holding hands as they had during their first kiss. Local legends suggest that Naka Cave serves as the final sanctuary for these lovers.

Snake Rock

The Naka or Naga cave bears physical characteristics that evoke the legend and its tragic conclusion. It gathers geological evidence that bolsters the myth's credibility. The cave's rocks exhibit textures resembling snake scales, layered across the entire surface. Inside, the cave walls are adorned with minerals emitting a glow like reptilian bellies. Moreover, certain stones have crystallized, adopting the form of a snake's head.

Geologists offer an explanation for the reptilian texture of the rocks, attributing it to significant temperature fluctuations between night and day. These variations cause the stone to contract and expand, consequently forming the distinct scale-like structure. Additionally, the cyclic process or erosion by water followed by drying further emphasizes the appearance of scales on the rock surfaces.

The love story between Prince Fahoong and Princess Nakkarintrani represents an enduring, classic tale: an impossible love between individuals from opposing clans, culminating in a tragic ending reminiscent of a Shakespearean tragedy. It stands as a poignant and beautiful love story, despite the foretold doom of the lovers. The princess, despite all her efforts, could not deny her true nature, even with her devoted energy. In love, as in life, the essence of who we are remains unchanged. While we may evolve or shed our old skin, our fundamental nature always persists.

The World Compass, September 2010

14.

THE TRUTH ABOUT LIES

1994

Several evenings per week, the family's home buzzes with visitors who come to engage with Marc. Initially, they encourage his involvement in the municipal council, then urge him to step up as a candidate in the by-elections. Ultimately, the kitchen transforms into the hub for his campaign as a councilor.

In his imagination, Jean-Philippe envisions himself participating in highly strategic meetings, with a map in the center of the table and figurative pawns that can be moved like in war movies. Unfortunately, Ithaca-on-the-Lake doesn't engage in conflict with any other city. His "war effort" revolves around distributing leaflets in the neighborhood to promote Marc's candidacy. Jean-Philippe runs from one mailbox to another, channeling his boundless energy. Hoping to spend more time with his father, he quickly realizes the opposite is taking place. Marc abandons their evening reading sessions, even though Jean-Philippe seeks that time together despite already reading novels on his own. Jean-Philippe had looked forward to starting *The Adventures of Tom Sawyer* together with his father, only to find himself reading alone.

> He had had a nice, good, idle time all the while—plenty of company—and the fence had three coats of whitewash on it! If he hadn't run out of whitewash, he would have bankrupted every boy in the village.
>
> Tom said to himself that it was not such a hollow world, after all. He had discovered a great law of human action, without knowing it—namely, that in order to make a man or a boy covet a thing, it is only necessary to make the thing difficult to attain.

Tom Sawyer managed to get others to paint the fence simply by changing the perspective. What a genius! Thanks to his charisma, the work was carried out simply because of the attraction it presented, and all the children wanted to be part of the chore. Jean-Philippe decides to try the strategy on his parents.

"If you want a scooter, you'll have to buy it yourself," says Marc.

"Where am I supposed to find the money? Nobody hires a fourteen-year-old like me," he complains.

"Go and leave your name at the grocery store; they're looking for baggers. Otherwise, it means you're too young to have a scooter."

"That'll take forever. You don't understand. You wouldn't have to come and take me to my friends' houses anymore. That's an advantage, don't you think?"

"Felix paid for his car; you can ask him to drive you back."

"Never mind. I prefer to figure it out on my own."

Jean-Philippe storms out of the kitchen and heads to his bedroom, slamming the door so hard the hinges vibrate.

"What did I tell you about slamming the door? Next time, I'll remove it. If you still want your privacy, you're going to stop that right now. Do you hear me?" shouts Marc from the bottom of the stairs.

Everything for Felix, nothing for you. There is clearly something you haven't understood.

Throughout his adolescence, Jean-Philippe demands everything: the right to go out, pocket money, and control over school night hours. His defiance of the household rules escalates, particularly when Felix provokes discussions by taunting him with his car trips, further worsening the atmosphere.

After the ban on shouting or slamming the door, Jean-Philippe begins to write stories. He's increasingly interested in crafting imaginary universes, depicting characters, and guiding their development. His days are therefore limited to reading, writing, and masturbating. He collects photos of men cut out from magazines or catalogs, storing them discreetly beneath his mattress. Preferring the male physique to the female, he harbors a secret fascination. In the black-and-white advertisement featuring Calvin Klein underwear, he daydreams of caressing Marky Mark's muscles.

He writes stories as a way to purge his emotions, yet he keeps them to himself. He writes dark and explosive stories to dispel his frustrations and fears while indulging in fantasies and dreams. He finds amusement in his own jokes and concocts various scenarios to kill his brother, who becomes his favorite target. In these stories, Felix has been tortured, buried alive, devoured by a giant spider, and abducted by aliens, just to name a few of his fates.

At his high school, the Odyssey, Jean-Philippe participates in a writing competition. This marks the first time he has shared a piece of writing with readers beyond himself. He submits his story titled "Steven and the Detective," depicting the journey of an orphan in search of his biological family. Ultimately, he clinches the first prize in the twelve- to fourteen-year-old category and witnesses the publication of his text in the regional newspaper.

Michelle celebrates her son's accomplishment, yet Marc doesn't even comment, causing Jean-Philippe to feel a sense of revolt. Michelle attempts to excuse Marc's silence, mentioning his new role as the replacement for the mayor after the previous one's resignation and his responsibilities with various matters. She assures Jean-Philippe that she'll arrange for Marc to read the story, but Jean-Philippe never hears back about "Steven and the Detective."

Consumed by sorrow and disappointment, he stops writing and throws his notebooks and his competition recognition certificate in the trash.

1996

For Jean-Philippe's sixteenth birthday, Marc arranges a room for him in the basement of the house. His parents intend to provide him with a personal space furnished with an armchair, a television, and a sound system. Jean-Philippe already works Thursday and Friday evenings as well as Saturdays at the village's grocery store. Marc has been re-elected to the position of mayor of Ithaca-on-the-Lake, a position that requires a lot of time and energy in the rapidly expanding municipality.

Instead of purchasing the scooter he'd desired, Jean-Philippe choses to invest his savings in a high-end Louis Garneau bicycle, along with suitable shoes, a helmet, shorts, and a yellow jersey adorned with images of the Tour de France. He spends his summers traveling hundreds of kilometers on country roads, feeling content far from the family home.

He also spends a lot of time with Daniel. When he isn't working at the grocery store, his group of friends gathers in

Daniel's basement, listening to music, playing Nintendo 64, and engaging in smoking pot and drinking. Daniel puts on music, specifically to please his girlfriend, Jessica, with songs from artists like Mariah Carey and Roxette echoing through the room. In this setting, at Daniel's place, he feels content, surrounded by friends, without anyone present to bother or upset him.

"I can't believe your parents don't say anything," remarks Jean-Philippe.

"It's cool. My parents prefer to see me here; they believe they're in control, so they let me have my experiences. My dad enjoys smoking too, so he takes advantage of it. He imagines that he's still sixteen years old," he explains with a laugh.

Jean-Philippe says, "My mother initially said, 'We're going to set up your room in the basement, so you can have your own private space!' But not long after, she complained, 'Your music is too loud! Turn down the sound!' It's pathetic. It's not the same freedom as I have here!"

Daniel turns up the volume to listen to Alanis Morissette's "Ironic." It feels like the singer wrote the song thinking about the relationship between Jean-Philippe and his mother.

1997

The following summer, Jean-Philippe rides his bicycle toward the neighboring village and stops at the edge of the pond. He sits down at the picnic table to cool off and eat a granola bar and a handful of nuts. Sitting on the table, with his feet on the bench, he watches some ducks swimming amid the tall grass. Two weeks earlier, he'd met a cyclist named David who, like him, traveled the main provincial roads.

"Do you know which village that is?" David asked, pointing behind Jean-Philippe.

"Yes, it's Ithaca-on-the-Lake," he replied, facing him.

"Okay! I see! I took a lot of winding roads, and I wasn't sure."

"And if you turn at the lights, you can ride toward the St. Penelope reservoir. If you like climbing, you should enjoy it. There are quite a few hills. Quite a challenge!"

"Thank you, I'll keep that in mind. You seem to know the area well."

"I live in Ithaca. This is my usual route."

"Are you training? For running or long distance?"

"Not really. Just for fun. I enjoy riding on the open road."

"You have the thighs and calves for riding long distances. By the way, I'm David."

"I'm Jean-Philippe," he said, shaking his hand.

David took large gulps from his flask while Jean-Philippe looked down, observing the cyclist's physique. Suddenly, he imagined himself transforming into a flask.

He's handsome, with those broad, square shoulders. That smirk too. And let's not even start on his butt and thighs! Stop staring; he'll think you're a total creep!

This big, athletic, curly-haired guy not only impressed him physically, but also emotionally. It was the first time he'd felt an attraction toward another man.

Jean-Philippe ardently wishes to see him again, and just the thought of it makes his face flush with heat.

You should've asked for his phone number, and you could've cycled together. But you're so stupid that it didn't even cross your mind. Too embarrassed!

Throughout the summer, Jean-Philippe frequents the pond but never encounters David again. He lives out his fantasies, envisioning romantic and intimate encounters with the attractive cyclist before drifting off to sleep.

"By the way, I'm David," continues to echo in his mind. He focuses on the masculine tone in David's words, recalling the sound of his voice and the way his lips moved. His thoughts linger on every place he imagines being kissed: the neck, the earlobe, the forehead, and especially the lips. Visualizing his own hands, he fantasizes about touching David's stomach, arms, shoulders, and buttocks. Lacking experience in this realm, he can only imagine the sensations, grappling alone with his desires and with no one to confide in. He yearns to be desired by another man and longs to experience love.

Your Prince Charming isn't in Ithaca-on-the-Lake. Do you really think a man like that would appear in such a hick town?

As he enters his home, a sense of melancholy overwhelms him. He loves men and struggles intensely to bury these feelings in a locked box deep in his mind.

It's settled; we won't talk about it anymore.

Daniel spends his evenings passionately kissing Jessica. Out of conscience or pity, Jessica introduces her best friend Laura to Jean-Philippe so that the four friends can spend their evenings together.

Jean-Philippe kisses Laura and caresses her breasts, as he has seen Daniel do with his girlfriend. She takes the opportunity to rub his penis through his pants. Surprisingly, the sensation delights him although it's disconcerting, especially when Laura undoes the button of the jeans and puts her hand in his boxers. He closes his eyes and lets the emotions rise.

Why do you imagine David's hand?

The following week, Jean-Philippe quickly introduces Laura to his parents before going down to the basement.

"The door must remain open," cautions Michelle.

Laura reassures her, "Don't worry, Ms. Genest, we won't do anything inappropriate."

In the bedroom, Laura reclines on the bed while Jean-Philippe takes a seat in his armchair. They engage in a conversation about cinema, prompted by the movie posters adorning the walls. Jean-Philippe points to a world map above his bed, sharing the travel destinations he hopes to visit. In contrast, Laura envisions spending a week in Cuba or the Dominican Republic. Jean-Philippe offers a polite smile and redirects the conversation to a different topic.

As a master of deception, he skillfully maneuvers through falsehoods. He tells his mother that he listens to music at Daniel's house, omitting the fact that his parents supply the beer and marijuana.

When he gets home, Michelle always says the same sentence to him, "Go wash yourself, you stink."

"Okay. We were doing work at Daniel's house."

"Daniel's house must be clean. I hope you have some energy left to clean your room!" she says sarcastically.

He takes off his clothes and buries them in the bottom of the laundry basket or offers to do a load of laundry.

One Saturday evening, however, Daniel and Jean-Philippe prepare some shots for their friends. After consuming about ten cocktails, which include a mixture of schnapps, vodka, and rum, Jean-Philippe starts feeling dizzy. And it begins to affect his stomach. When he's riding his bike home in the middle of the night, his unsteady cycling makes his heartburn even worse. He opens the door to the house and moves cautiously, trying to be silent, but he stumbles against the furniture in his way. In doing so, he accidentally knocks over the large plant while attempting to grasp one of the sword-shaped leaves of the sansevieria. As he reaches the bathroom on the ground floor, he starts to feel nauseous.

Upon hearing the sounds of vomiting, his father and mother wake up.

"It can't be! What have you done now?" his mother exclaims. "You're far too young to be drinking. I'm going to speak to Daniel's parents! You won't be going to his place anymore. He's a bad influence on you. This doesn't make any sense. When are you going to grow up? I hope nobody saw you. This is not going to reflect well on us!"

Marc intervenes, saying, "Michelle, go back to bed, I'll take care of it."

Watch out, here comes the sermon. "Your brother would never have done that," and "You should follow in his footsteps."

"He can eat shit! He's not a role model!" Jean-Philippe exclaims, apparently without providing any context for his statement.

"I'm going to place a damp towel around your neck to help you cool down," Marc says calmly.

"Everything is spinning so fast. I feel like it's going to come out again," he says, leaning over the toilet bowl.

Marc does his best to assist his son within the confined space of the small bathroom on the first floor. He supports his son's head over the bowl, provides a glass of water for him to clean his mouth, and wipes his lips after spitting into the bowl.

Jean-Philippe lies down on the cool bathroom tiles, finding comfort in the freshness. Marc helps his son back to his bed and disinfects the bathroom before returning to his own bed.

You can shout that you're gay, a faggot, a degenerate. You can shout it because nobody hears you... You're too stupid, too afraid to accept yourself as you are. Keep hiding. Act as if nothing happened. You're invisible because you decided to hide. You like men... So, go hide out in Montreal. Go ahead, run away...

15.

PERSONAL LANDSLIDE

April 2010

Jean-Philippe rearranges the furniture in the living room according to Michelle's wishes, and this time, she takes the role of a director rather than a decorator, prioritizing utility over embellishment. Marc comes home to spend his last weeks in his own house, in his village. Doctors had tried in vain to keep him in the hospital, but like everything else, his stubbornness won out.

Felix found a bed that can be adjusted to different positions, and Jean-Philippe moves the bed in front of the bay window. Michelle hangs opaque curtains to reduce the overly bright light since the living room has become Marc's bedroom.

To declutter the room, Jean-Philippe transports an armchair, decorative tables, and a few plants to the basement.

A nurse came earlier to meet Michelle, provide her with information about basic care, and give her the list of medications and their dosages. For the remainder, the nurse will visit Marc several times a week.

With Easter now behind them, this April morning brings cool and cloudy weather. Michelle and Jean-Philippe put on windbreakers to welcome Marc outside. He sits in the wheelchair that Felix borrowed to ease his transport into the house, wrapped in a blanket to ward off the cold, even though the distance isn't very far. Marc is wearing his Montreal Expos tuque, the same one he's had for twenty years, if not more.

Jean-Philippe joins Felix to help him carry his father to the balcony.

"Move aside," says Felix. "I know how to do it. I can do it on my own."

You're a wimp, a weakling. He must think you're still eight years old... or just a poof!

"I can help, you know. If you knew all the equipment we carry in the mountains, you'd be surprised."

"I'm sorry. But it's definitely going to be easier on my own. I have my techniques, and this isn't my first time. You can take the bag from the trunk of the car."

"Are you sure?"

"Yes. Really."

Jean-Philippe hesitantly lets go of the wheels in front of the chair. He doesn't doubt Felix's strength, but he still wants to avoid his father's unexpected fall.

After removing all his winter clothes, Felix helps Marc get into bed while Jean-Philippe places his bag and his belongings in the foyer.

"Mom, if you need anything, you know I'm not far away. You just have to call me," Felix says.

"I'm here. I can take care of everything. I can go shopping and stop by the pharmacy. I can even do the washing," replies Jean-Philippe.

"I know you're there. But right now, Mom and Dad are counting on you. Are you going to be up to the task? Can I trust you?"

"I think I'll get through this!" Jean-Philippe counters.

Felix kisses his mother on both cheeks and says good-bye to his father before leaving. Installed in the corner of the living room, Marc has a view of the outside, of the television and the family photos with the kitchen and the bathroom nearby. Despite his fatigue, he smiles. He sighs with relief as he lays his head on the pillow. He tries the buttons on the bed's remote control, which is much more sophisticated than the hospital one. He knows that returning home will put pressure on his wife, but Jean-Philippe's presence reassures him. He has promised them that he's willing to return to St. Menelaus if and when it becomes too difficult for them.

Marc crushes crackers into his soup to thicken it, making it easier to swallow with a more solid consistency due to his limited ability to eat.

In the kitchen, Jean-Philippe puts away the plates that are still hot from the dishwasher, and he finds himself thinking about Rahim, who appreciates tidying up. Rahim would be proud of him. He then joins his father in the living room.

He pushes the scattered papers and books to take a seat on the couch. He places his cell phone on his lap to catch up on his *World Compass* emails. His editor has sent notes for the report from Northern Ireland. Later, in the evening, he'll rework his text when his parents are asleep. The silence at the start of the night brings a meditative and productive atmosphere that Jean-Philippe cherishes.

"I brought in the internet! I hope you don't mind?" asks Jean-Philippe.

"You know me and technology. We equipped everyone at the town hall. We changed the computers, but hey, I still like having my paper documents."

"You would have been good with the Mennonites!"

"I'm not sure. I like my car and my television. What are you currently working on?" asks his father.

"The Giant's Causeway. The text should appear at the beginning of summer. I also have two more in production."

"They must be proud of your work, I can tell. Getting a monthly column with a guaranteed salary—impressive. A local guy like you writing for a prestigious magazine in London, and in English to top it off. It's quite an accomplishment! The folks in the village will be thrilled to hear about it!"

His parents' pride has always been proportional to the speed of transmission of the news in the village.

"I believe so. At least, I've received mostly positive feedback. Not everything I write is a masterpiece, but with a little effort, you can produce something decent. My mentor, Jerry, used to say, 'As long as there's red ink, it's a good sign!' "

"Why does he say that?"

"There's always work to be done on a text. It's never really over. If your article comes back blank, you screwed up, and you have to start from scratch."

"I'm sure it's good."

"We need to adapt to the demands of the publishing world. That's why there are people who review the text. Sometimes we become so immersed in our subject that we assume it's understood, but it may not be clear. Upon rereading, we adjust based on the feedback. That's what I'll be working on this evening."

"I knew you were good in English. Speaking is one thing, but writing it is another. Doesn't that discourage you sometimes?"

"At first, I saw corrections as criticism, something negative. So, I started studying and understanding the subtleties of English. But in reality, it's never perfect, and you have to accept that."

Just then, Marc's spoon falls to the living room floor, and the bowl of soup spills onto the bed before joining the utensil on the floor. Marc is unable to speak or breathe. He places his hand on his neck and looks at Jean-Philippe with eyes that cry out for help.

Jean-Philippe quickly rises from his seat and rushes to the bed. Uncertain about what to do, he realizes that his mother is at the grocery store and won't be back for at least half an hour.

"Are you able to cough?" he asks.

Without a response, Jean-Philippe must act quickly. His father's airway is blocked. He advances to his father and vigorously slaps him on the back, but without success. He turns him on his side, his head out of the bed hoping that the piece stuck in his airway will go back in the opposite direction by gravity. Jean-Philippe continues to punch his father in the back. He can't do the Heimlich maneuver on him; his father's stomach still has the stitches from his operation. Marc's body loses vigor and his face changes color.

If he dies, you're screwed. You're going to blame yourself for it all your life. He belongs in the hospital, not here! Life can't end with a piece of cracker in the throat. You still need time. Hit, hit, hit.

A gooey ball of flour finally falls to the ground. Marc starts breathing again. He coughs and spits saliva on the ground, his head still upside down. Jean-Philippe rubs his back to comfort him.

"Are you okay? Are you ready to get up? I know I mistreated you," said Jean-Philippe.

With his hoarse voice, Marc replies, "Yes, it's fine."

Jean-Philippe helps his father get back into bed and Marc inhales deeply, as if the air were filling him for the first time. He coughs and spits into a tissue.

"Don't scare me like that anymore, do you hear me?"

Jean-Philippe's heart is pumping blood to his head as if he'd run a marathon. He leans against the wall and slides to the floor, curling up into a little ball, knees pressed against his shoulders.

“Do you want me to call the hospital? The ambulance? The nurse?” he asks.

“No. Don't call anyone,” his father insists.

“Someone will have to come and check if I haven't caused any damage, if the stitches in your wound are still holding, and if I haven't hurt you.”

“No. I'm fine.”

“Well, things aren't going well. Are you sure you wouldn't be better off in the hospital? Did you think about Mom if she’d been here?”

“Exactly; she’s not here. There’s no question of me going back to the hospital. My place is here, and I won't move.”

“Damn, you have a hard head!”

“The same as you. When you have something in your head, you don't have it in your ass!”

The short silence, confused and questioning, is shattered by a burst of laughter. Jean-Philippe collapses on the ground because he’s laughing so hard. In the release of adrenaline, tears stream down his cheeks, blurring the line between laughter and relief. His father starts laughing while holding his stomach and Jean-Philippe emits a contended sigh.

“But what are we going to tell Mom?” asks Jean-Philippe, looking at the overturned bowl of soup.

“We’ll say that I dropped the bowl, that's all.”

“She's going to suspect something. We need to change the sheets and your clothes. At least you didn't get burned.”

“No, I don’t think so. Anyway, I don't feel anything.”

“I'll clean it up before Mom comes back. Otherwise, you know her, she’ll worry.”

“It's a secret between the two of us. You don't say anything to your mother.”

"It's okay. I'll take your bowl to the sink and come back with a rag. You're worse than a child."

"I guess we're swapping roles," says Marc.

Michelle kisses Marc before going up to her room. Jean-Philippe closes his laptop.

"Me too, I'm going down to my room. It was a big day," he says, looking at his father with a half-smile.

"Stay with me for a while, please."

"Just a bit, then I'm turning off the television and we're going to sleep," he says, smiling at Marc.

"Tell me, have you ever considered coming back to Quebec?" questions Marc. "There are journalists who do great work here."

"I did consider it, especially during the first year in London. In my mind, I was just going to be a year abroad, and then I had to come up with a plan for my return to Quebec. But things changed quickly. The demand for reporters at *World Compass* allowed me to work full time. Amy and I got assignments all over the world. The magazine has never been more popular, and they're even developing shows for the BBC. It's a significant opportunity. I won't run out of work, and I genuinely enjoy it. I feel like I belong and that I'm making a difference. Maybe I'll ask them to send me to North America more often, so I can spend more time with you."

"I saw that you started reading again. Your books are still in the library downstairs."

"Yes, I've immersed myself in *The Odyssey*, by Homer. You know, the Ancient Greeks. It's still incredible how books can teach us about ourselves. You can take an excerpt and find meaning in it, and that meaning can vary from person to person. It always depends on where we are in our life, what we understand about our reality, and our identity. I've long said that *Around the World in Eighty Days* was a pivotal book for me. I wouldn't be who I am today without it. It came into my life during my youth and played a significant role in inspiring my career in exploration and writing. Now, I find myself recreating the adventures of Jules Verne."

"When I read it to you, I also found myself in the story, although it remained a mere dream. I would have liked to take risks like the English character, whose name I can't recall…"

"Phileas Fogg," Jean-Philippe reminds him.

"Exactly, taking trips, going on a whim. We agree that with a family, it's more difficult to do so. But it got me thinking. I changed jobs to be closer to you. Then I took on the position of mayor. These were significant changes, and they were stressful. Like Phileas Fogg, I launched myself without a safety net. This meant I had to work a lot to make it work. My own risk also involved my family."

"Today, rereading *The Odyssey*, I interpret the story differently than I did at eighteen. I'll read you an excerpt.

'They started at once, and went about among the Lotus-eaters, who did them no hurt, but gave them to eat of the lotus, which was so delicious that those who ate of it left off caring about home, and did not even want to go back and say what had happened to them, but were for staying and munching lotus with the Lotus-eaters without thinking further of their return; nevertheless, though they wept bitterly I forced them back to the ships and made them fast under the benches. Then I told the rest to go on board at once, lest any of them should taste of the lotus and leave off wanting to get home, so they took their places and smote the grey sea with their oars.'

"As a teenager, I imagined the lotus as a drug, something you can't stop craving, something you can't stop consuming. At thirty years old, I reflect on the reasons why the crew used the lotus. They forgot their torment but above all, they neglected the desire to return home. When I was younger, I sought refuge in alcohol and pot because I didn't accept who I was. As a man, I found myself still concealing everything. I immersed myself in work; it provided me with a reason to avoid returning here. I turned away from memories, from my past. I've built a fortress around myself, and no one is able to penetrate it."

"That's not a life. And it feels like it was us, your parents, who pushed you into this."

"Yes. No. Maybe. I don't know anymore. I've been angry at you for a long time. I've blamed you for all my misfortunes since I was a teenager. Even as an adult, I held you responsible for all the wrongs and the reasons for my suffering. I had to leave, to find myself. I had to move to a different continent to grow, to understand who I was without you. It was upon my return that I realized I'm me because of you, in both my joys and sorrows. I am Jean-Philippe Genest, son of Michelle and Marc Genest because now I understand that the obstacles, pitfalls, and barriers will always be there, whether with or against me. But if I'm able to rise again, it's because I had your support, your guidance, and your love, despite the obstacles and the troubles."

Jean-Philippe closes his notebook and picks up his papers scattered on the sofa. There is a peaceful atmosphere in the living room that calms everyone's spirits.

Marc finally dares to speak. "I would like you to take care of your mother when I'm gone," he murmurs serenely.

"That's why you wanted to talk to me?"

"She doesn't say it, but I'm afraid she feels alone. You know she always worries about everything."

"Yes, I know. Do you remember when I came out? Mom was so stressed."

"Those weren't our finest moments, I must admit. No one teaches us how to react when we receive that kind of news. I look back, and I realize we weren't great with you."

2003

Jean-Philippe borrows his roommate's old Toyota Tercel to drive to Ithaca-on-the-Lake. In exchange, he brings back meals cooked by his mother, which he shares with his roommates. These are simple meals but oh, so comforting, and they're always appreciated by everyone.

He parks behind his father's car in the driveway and enters quickly, causing his mother to jump.

"Don't surprise me like that!" Michelle says, walking toward her son to kiss him on the cheeks. "You're just in time for lunch."

"I know. I do it on purpose to get a free meal," he jokes.

Marc walks up from the basement with his t-shirt covered in sawdust and squeezes his son's shoulders to show his joy.

"Finally, you show your face!" he says as he goes to the sink. "You'll have to go to the hairdresser. You're starting to have long hair."

"I'm going to let it grow. I think it suits me well. And what about you? Have you been doing some carpentry?"

"Yes. Working with my hands helps me clear my mind."

Marc washes his hands, and they sit down at the table while Michelle reheats the leftover salmon pie from the day before.

"We're working to block the establishment of a strip club next to the marina. It's not easy. We don't want that kind of establishment here. We want the waterfront to be family-friendly, so there's no question of giving them a permit. We're concerned it will attract bikers and people drinking, which isn't what we want."

"You have a lot of prejudices!"

"Traditionally, this is a town of farmers. We have a few businesses that have come to set up shops and the village has grown, but the people come here for the peace and quiet. It's not a party town."

"I imagine the neighbors spying to see if they know someone coming in or out of the bar! That would cause a lot of gossip."

“You can call me old-fashioned; the fact remains that I don't really like disturbance.”

Michelle places plates of salmon pie in front of her husband and son. She makes herself a ham sandwich. She hates eating the same meal two days in a row. “It lacks creativity,” she says.

The Genests enjoy a strong reputation in the community, with their neighbors holding them in high regard. Marc takes pride in decorating the house for Halloween, Christmas, or St. John the Baptist Day, while Michelle tends to a lovely flower garden whose colors change along the summer season. All the passers-by greet them in the street. During Felix's college years, they proudly supported his football team and celebrated his championships. Following in his parents’ footsteps, Felix now serves as a police officer and is married to a local girl named Julie. They have one daughter, with another on the way. Meanwhile, Jean-Philippe has taken an atypical academic path. He initially pursued geography but later switched to literature and communication.

“Mom, Dad, I have something to tell you. I've been thinking about this for a long time. Maybe that's why I haven't been in contact with you lately. It’s true that there was work. It's also true that I was trying to tell you things that aren’t easy to say, so I was always delaying. I think you have the right to know the truth, so that there are no barriers between us.”

He takes a deep breath before throwing the bomb.

“Mom, Dad, I’m gay,” he blurts dryly.

A silence settles in the kitchen. No one speaks or moves. Marc freezes, fork in hand.

“Are you okay?” he asks after a few seconds of silence.

Michelle gets up and walks toward the kitchen counter. She takes the glass pot from the coffee maker to fill it with water.

"Are you going to have coffee? Marc?" she asks.

Jean-Philippe feels quite unsettled. For several weeks, he has had trouble sleeping, preparing himself for the various possible reactions from his parents. In the worst-case scenario, he feared being kicked out, but he knew that wasn't in his parents' nature. He would have preferred to see an outburst, tears, or any kind of response, but above all, not silence. Knowing that his parents have rather traditional views, Jean-Philippe had played a role to ensure they didn't suspect his true orientation.

All his friends have stories of coming out, some more convoluted than others. His won't go down in history.

"Mom, it's okay. You have the right to react, to not be happy."

"Please, let us have time to process this!" Marc replies. "You've surprised us by dropping this on us, and we need some time to collect our thoughts. I thought you were going to tell us about a new job or a move. We just need to put our ideas in order. Give us some time, please."

"Exactly. I'm here so we can talk about it together."

"Do many people know about you?" asks Michelle. "Before us, I mean?"

"There are my friends in Montreal; that's pretty much it. But within the family, you're the first I've talked to about it."

"We'll need to figure out how to tell your uncles, aunts, and your brother. However, at the same time, it's really none of their business," she says hesitantly.

"You don't have to justify yourself. You have nothing to hide. You're right; it's none of their business."

"That's easy for you to say. You're not the one who lives here. There's going to be more talk, and we're going to have to find a way to explain that," says Marc.

"Explain what? It's 2003. I'm twenty-three years old. It's everywhere on television. It's almost normal."

"Normal, normal. You're the one who says it. Maybe in the big city, but not in Ithaca-on-the-Lake. You know, it's pretty conservative here."

"That means you won't have children, no family. You're going to be alone all your life. That's not a life. Are you sure?" asks Michelle.

"Sure of what? That I'm gay? Well, yes. There is no doubt. I wanted to make myself believe that I could be bisexual, but I have no attraction to women. It's not me. And I won't be alone all my life. I hope to have a lover one day."

"Look, you're always welcome in our house, but there's no way you're bringing a boyfriend with you. You're my boy, but I'm not sure I could handle seeing you kiss another man or hold his hand. There's no way you're doing that in front of your niece. She's just a child. No, no, she's not ready for that," Marc expresses his concerns.

"What difference does it make that I'm gay?"

"But it changes everything! You don't understand that we gave you everything. We raised you. You didn't lack anything. I worked hard to ensure that we had a town for families. I thought you'd settle here, with your wife and children, but you decided to live in Montreal because it was easier to travel. We didn't say anything and meanwhile, you were having sex with other... Well, you know what I mean."

"Other guys?" Jean-Philippe prods.

"Yeah, that's it! Have you thought about all the sacrifices we've made all these years?"

"So I shouldn't be gay because you paid for my education. That's it?"

"Well, no, big doofus," says Marc. He picks up crumbs from the pie to keep his hands busy.

Michelle cries silently while standing near the kitchen counter.

Well done! You made your mother cry!

"Why are you crying, Mom?"

"Because I'm worried that you might face a life of hardship. Not everyone is accepting of gay people, and there are those who will judge you, and by extension, us. I can already hear them, saying hurtful things, like 'Look at her, not capable of raising her boy like everyone else.' "

"Fuck them! You don't have to go through that."

"It's easier said than done. We have to live with them. When you leave, you're going to return to your gang of homosexuals in the big city. It's not the same here. You may have had time to get used to it, but it's hitting us like a ton of bricks. So, we might not be as happy as you'd hoped."

"We're an hour from Montreal. You can't make me believe that people won't understand!"

"When you said you had a girlfriend, you were lying to us, right?"

"Lying isn't the right word... I lied to you, I lied to myself..."

“You see, if you’d been honest earlier, we wouldn't be here today.”

“Would that have been better?” asks Jean-Philippe.

“When you leave, your life continues, but ours stops. Well, it changes, and I don’t like changes…”

16.

MOTHER GODDESS

April 2010

"Hey, Babe!"

"Wow! Rahim! It's quite a surprise for you to call me at this time. I hope everything's going well at the office."

"I guess everything is fine. I really don't know; I'm not in the office," he says, his voice laced with nervousness.

"How so? Where are you?" asks Jean-Philippe.

"I'm in Montreal! I'm at the airport. I wanted to surprise you, and I wanted to see you."

"At the airport? In Montreal? Right now?"

"Yes, I arrived safely! You know I'm not an impulsive man, and I don't know what happened, but I bought a ticket to Montreal and here I am," he explains, a tremor in his voice. "But now, you have to come and pick me up or tell me how to get to you. I'm feeling a bit overwhelmed, and I don't really know what to do at the moment. First of all, I'm glad you answered the phone."

"Listen carefully. You're going to wait for me at the airport. You're going to sit in a small café; there are a few on the Arrivals side. You're going to text me the name of the place, and I'm going to meet you there. I'll be there in about an hour if there isn't too much traffic. Don't worry, I'm coming."

In shock, Jean-Philippe hangs up the phone and looks at his parents without really knowing what to say or do.

"Can I take the car?" he asks.

"What's happening? Is everything okay?" asks Michelle.

"It's Rahim. He wanted to surprise me, and he just landed in Montreal."

"That's a nice surprise!"

"You don't understand. This is very big, what's happening. Rahim is genuinely a good guy, but he's incredibly anxious. Extremely so. Someday, I'll share his story with you. However, the fact that he took a flight, alone, without prior notice, is unheard of. He had to overcome immense stress to make this happen."

"It's love, my boy," Marc says. "Don't keep him waiting; bring him back here. We can't wait to meet him."

Like a child at Christmas time faced with too many presents, he doesn't know where to turn. Sitting on the floor, he puts on his shoes like a six-year-old and then leaves like a rocket toward the car. However, he returns immediately; he has forgotten to take the keys.

2008

Two months after the start of their relationship, Rahim decides to introduce Jean-Philippe to his family during a weekend in the countryside. The estate, located more than two hours from London, belonged to the Strands for generations. When Jean-Philippe was young, he dreamed of owning a cabin in the woods, but the Strand country house is more like a castle than a cabin in the north. As Rahim drives his BMW through the two sculpted columns, the metallic doors open automatically, and Jean-Philippe feels a burst of heat on his cheeks as the imposing estate comes into view. Rahim places his hand on Jean-Philippe's arm.

"Don't be impressed by everything you see. My family will love you. They're rather simple people," Rahim tries to reassure his lover.

What are you still doing here? You'll never be good enough for this family. This isn't your world. They're from another social class. You come from a small country village.

Jean-Philippe presses his nose against the car window, taking in the view of the avenue of elms that line the road leading to the house. He also admires the colorful flower beds and meticulously trimmed shrubs that enhance the manor's facade. Rahim parks the BMW in front of the garage, and Jean-Philippe is captivated by the Georgian architecture, where tawny and golden stones perfectly complement the lush greenery.

"Are you okay? Are you ready?"

Jean-Philippe emits a few rumbling noises, but only raises his hands and shoulders, a sign that he has no other choice but to follow Rahim. They get out of the car and retrieve their bags from the trunk. Jean-Philippe straightens the collar of his shirt under his sweater and pulls up his gray checked wool pants to smooth them out, a set he has bought in preparation for the weekend in the countryside. He runs his hands through his hair to tidy it up.

You look poor next to him.

Each with their bag in hand, Rahim takes his boyfriend's free hand as they head toward the front door. He kisses his lover's cheek before pushing the door open.

Jean-Philippe wears his biggest smile as he steps inside.

The immense hall, richly adorned with works of art, busts, and antique furniture, transports Jean-Philippe to another era. They're greeted by Yasmina, Rahim's sister, who is accompanied by her three-year-old son.

They leave their bag in the entrance.

"Rahim!" she exclaims, taking her son by the hand. "Ricky, come say hello to your uncle."

Rahim wraps his arms around his sister and bends down to pick up Ricky.

"You've grown up! You're going to be taller than me soon!"

Ricky kisses his uncle while Rahim tickles him. The laughter that fills the hall soothes Jean-Philippe's apprehensions.

"Mom, Rahim has arrived!" Yasmina shouts.

She approaches Jean-Philippe, who extends his hand to introduce himself.

"Come here so I can give you a kiss. We've heard so much about you that it feels like we already know you."

Yasmina hugs Jean-Philippe and, after the initial surprise, he hugs her back.

"I hope they were all good comments!" he says.

"Absolutely! The man who convinced Rahim to give up smoking deserves all my admiration."

"Is William here?" Rahim asks.

"No, he and Dad are on the golf course. They should be back for dinner. He never stops working, so when he can do a little sport, I let him go. Opportunities are rare. Sara is in the office upstairs. We'll go drag her out of work together; she'll be happy to see you. Mom shouldn't be long."

Rahim's mother arrives from the kitchen where she's supervising the meal preparations. When she enters, Rahim straightens his back and squares his shoulders instinctively. She opens her arms gracefully to kiss her son, who is a head taller than her.

"Did you have a good trip?" Veda asks.

"Of course! The weather was magnificent. Mother, let me introduce you to Jean-Philippe. This is my mother, Veda."

"Nice to meet you, madam."

"I'm very happy to finally meet you. Please, be welcome and make yourself at home," Veda replies warmly.

Rahim's mother is a lovely and very attractive woman. Rahim bears a resemblance to her, sharing her shiny black hair but having a paler complexion. Her smile illuminates the room, and it's hard to guess her age because she's so radiant.

"Do we leave the bags here?" asks Jean-Philippe.

"Yes, you can leave them for now. Rahim can show you around, and in the meantime, we'll serve tea on the terrace. Are you hungry?"

"Yes, I'm starving, and I think we've got a little man here who wouldn't say no to a cupcake. Right, Ricky?"

"A cake, a cake!" Ricky shouts, echoed by Rahim as they head outside.

Rahim winks at Jean-Philippe, who smiles in return as he follows Rahim. Rahim's relationship with Ricky reminds him of his nieces, and he finds himself missing them terribly.

Yasmina sets Ricky up with his trucks on the play mat spread out on the terrace. Sara joins the family and pours herself a glass of iced tea before taking a seat in the sunlight. Rahim, Jean-Philippe, and Veda settle in the shaded part of the terrace. Even in the heat, Rahim and his mother prefer their tea hot while Jean-Philippe opts for a large glass of cold water.

"Sitting at the office for too long, I miss the sun, so I take advantage of it," Sara remarks.

The two Strand sisters bear a striking resemblance to each other, except for their hair. Sara sports very short hair, while Yasmina's hair is longer, resembling her mother's. Sara is actively involved in the family business and has been taking more and more initiative to master all aspects of the company. Rahim and his sisters are the heirs of a multinational manufacturing hygiene products such as soaps, shampoos, and toothpaste.

Over the years, the European company has diversified and now has a presence in the Asian and American markets, offering a wide range of makeup products and various foods items. As a provider of everyday goods, Strand Corp. has steadily grown and thrived over the past century, even in the face of wars and economic recessions.

The Strands had considered Rahim as a potential successor to his father's position at the helm of the family business, but he ultimately chose a different path. During his youth, Rahim experienced a series of anxiety attacks that caused concern for his parents. They consulted numerous doctors, psychologists, and therapists in their quest to understand and help their son. At times, he even refused to eat or attend school, finding it impossible to leave the house. Fortunately, with the aid of medication and, more importantly, through therapy and exercises, he managed to regain a normal rhythm in his life. This progress allowed him to excel in school and pursue a job he's passionate about.

"It's partly my fault if Rahim didn't choose to work with his father."

Veda places her hand on her son's arm, and in her eyes, Jean-Philippe discerns all the motherly affection she feels for her son, even though she exudes a commanding matriarchal presence.

"It's my choice, Mother. You shouldn't burden yourself with blame. I'm genuinely happy with my job, and I wouldn't change a thing. Sara is doing an excellent job in the company, and Father couldn't have chosen a better successor."

"You're right," Veda says. "Sara is perfect for this role. She's a natural leader."

"I still have a long way to go," Sara replies modestly.

The matriarch adopts a solemn demeanor as she begins to recount the story of her family. Jean-Philippe can't help but be reminded of all the times his own mother tirelessly repeated family anecdotes. This inclination to narrate stories is a way of showcasing the lineage's heritage, the shared genetics of their common folklore, and their family mythology.

"You know, Jean-Philippe, my family in Mumbai is quite traditional, very committed to customs and religion. In India, it's an integral part of our daily life. And when you're born into a privileged family, while the vast majority of the country lives in poverty, my brothers, sisters, and I felt the need to work hard to maintain what we had. When Rahim was born, there were expectations, both in my family and his father's, for me to groom him to succeed Thomas. I asked for a lot and pushed my demands too far when he was at an age where the most important thing should have been playing and making friends. I didn't know how to strike the right balance in his upbringing."

Rahim turns to Jean-Philippe.

"All my days were meticulously planned down to the minute, and I had to absorb everything the teachers threw at us while maintaining grades that couldn't dip below excellence," Rahim explains. "I gave it my all, working evenings and weekends, but my young mind eventually broke down. I couldn't function anymore," he continues. "I spent weeks in tears, hiding, and not eating. I'd get angry and destroy everything around me."

"It's hard to imagine you like that. It's so different from your current personality," Jean-Philippe remarks.

"We consulted a pediatrician and ultimately, it was Dr. Kamerfield who arranged therapy for Rahim to help him cope with his stress. What did she call it? Performance anxiety?"

"Yes, exactly. In an extreme form."

"I was overprotective of him and had overly high expectations. I burdened myself with obligations that I passed on to him. Rahim felt all the fears I had for him."

"But as a teenager, things were already getting better," Rahim reassures her.

"You played a lot of sports and joined a cricket team in a league with friends your age, and it was around this time that you started sleeping better. We finally saw the light at the end of the tunnel."

"Now I understand your cricket fanaticism more," says Jean-Philippe.

"Mother used to take us to watch Rahim play cricket every weekend," Yasmina tells him.

"My mother used to take me to watch my brother play American football."

"And we preferred to have fun with our dolls. Sara, do you remember when we made castles in the stands?" Yasmina reminisces.

"I was drawing. I had a notebook and colored pencils," Jean-Philippe adds, laughing.

Yasmina pours some tea into her mother's and Rahim's cups, and then offers another glass of water to Jean-Philippe.

Rahim takes his mother's hand and kisses it. "I love you all the same, Mother. You did your best with the three of us and it turned out well," he reassures her.

She looks at him. "At university, you followed in your father's footsteps, but you chose finance over business management."

"I hesitated, but I felt the pressure to constantly outdo myself was still very much present within me. It made me physically ill. I didn't want to experience those feelings that took me back to my early adolescence and the dark days of panic attacks. For the sake of my well-being and for the good of the company as well, I told Father that I wouldn't work in the family business."

"How did he take it?" Jean-Philippe asks.

"Let's say we had a lengthy discussion, but I managed to make him see my perspective, and in the end, it was the right decision," Rahim replies.

"Yasmina clearly wasn't interested," Veda said.

"No, thank you!" Yasmina interjects.

"So, Sara seized the opportunity to announce that she wanted to work with her father and, over the months, she gradually joined the company. She's been there ever since," Veda adds.

After dinner, the whole family goes to the living room for a digestif. The menu prepared by the cook consisted of Mont Saint-Michel salt marsh lamb accompanied by root vegetables and a slightly spicy mint sauce. Everybody enjoyed it, and Jean-Philippe feels blessed to have taken part in this culinary delight. The spacious room, richly decorated, has two loveseats and two armchairs facing each other, surrounding a coffee table, which facilitates discussions. In the corner of the living room is an enormous bar where a series of crystal glasses line up in front of a mirror that reflects light in all directions.

Jean-Philippe charmed the entire clan at dinner with his travel stories, and Yasmina teased him about his French accent. Veda came to his defense, herself an Indian with a slight accent.

"I met Thomas at Oxford. I was there to study law, having received a scholarship which I'd started in Mumbai."

"What a magnificent city! I hope I'll have the opportunity to go back, with Rahim perhaps?" says Jean-Philippe.

"I went there twice to meet Mother's family. I warn you right away, traveling isn't the easiest thing. With my anxiety, it takes a lot of preparation."

"I'll be there for you," reassures Jean-Philippe.

Thomas offers Jean-Philippe a glass of scotch, which he cannot refuse. Like a child preparing to unwrap a gift, he inhales the smoky and fruity aromas, closing his eyes to savor the moment.

"I hope you enjoy it. A Bowmore, twenty-five years old," Thomas informs him.

"Mr. Strand, I never thought one day I would be able to taste a scotch of this quality. You have no idea how grateful I am."

"A connoisseur! Call me Thomas, please. Rahim's friends are my friends. You're welcome in our home. Come on, have a taste."

Jean-Philippe sips the scotch and notes a taste of caramel and hazelnuts. The succession of flavors in the mouth makes the experience exhilarating.

"Wow!" he says, letting his emotions rise.

"I knew you would like it," Rahim whispers, taking his hand.

Jean-Philippe approaches Rahim to whisper in his ear. "Thank you for these beautiful moments. I love you," he says for the first time with the certainty of understanding true love.

"Me too, Babe," he says with a wink.

Rahim takes advantage of the rapprochement to kiss him on the forehead, and Jean-Philippe savors his scotch again.

Yasmina returns to the living room after putting Ricky to bed. She sits on the armrest of William's chair and wraps her arm around him.

"It's been a long time since I've seen my brother this happy. It's obvious there's a connection between the two of you. Not that I want to put pressure on you, but it's reassuring to see your complicity," says Yasmina. "What was your ex's name, the one who was at our wedding?" she asks her brother.

"Scott."

"Yes, that's it, Scott," she confirms, sighing. "My God, he gave you a hard time. He exploited you and lied to your face and you saw nothing. Didn't he steal from you too? My brother is a good guy, kind and generous. He didn't understand that Scott was manipulating him," she says, looking at Jean-Philippe. "It was me who intervened with Rahim so that he would open his eyes and realize his ex's actions."

"After the separation, he tried to call me back. He called several times a day, but it wasn't until after the breakup that I really learned everything he'd done. He was sleeping with other guys. He would take items from my house and resell them. In short, I felt exploited, manipulated, and humiliated."

"I can reassure you that my intentions are true," says Jean-Philippe. "I love Rahim more and more every day, and I know now that I probably have to be friends with Yasmina; otherwise, I'm going to have a bad time."

Everyone laughs at Jean-Philippe's joke, but he isn't wrong.

"What do your parents do in Quebec?" asks Veda.

"My father, Marc, is the mayor of the village, and my mother, Michelle, doesn't work outside the home. She stayed at home for me and my brother Felix. My brother's a police officer, and he has two daughters, Camille and Charlie. They're five and seven years old now."

"I admire his dedication. Politics, even at the municipal level, isn't given to everyone," says Thomas.

"And it isn't too difficult to be away from them?" Veda enquires.

"I talk to my mother every month. Since Felix and I left home, she's started doing a little volunteer work and she babysits her granddaughters occasionally. It's hard not seeing my nieces, but I call them from time to time. When I saw Ricky earlier with Rahim, I had a moment of nostalgia."

"I hope I get the chance to meet your mother one of these days. She must be a wonderful lady to have raised a handsome young man like you."

For Veda, this is the expression she uses to signify that she agrees to this relationship. Rahim understands immediately that Jean-Philippe has seduced his mother.

"Thank you very much. I sincerely hope so too."

"How did she take the fact that you're gay?" she asks bluntly.

"Mother! A little restraint, please," says Rahim.

"It's a normal subject. I spend my day with gays in the hospital. It's not like I'm asking him if he has a venereal disease!"

"Mother, stop that!"

Everybody laughs at the turn of the discussion. Jean-Philippe understands that Rahim's family lives in luxury, yet with simplicity. The family is a strong core, undoubtedly the most important thing for them, allowing them to keep their feet on the ground.

"I would say that it wasn't easy. In fact, they were surprised and didn't expect me to make this announcement. I come from a small country village, and they were afraid of gossip, of comments. They were uncomfortable with that information and didn't know how to deal with my identity, which they had to make their own. They were no longer just parents, they were parents of a gay child, and that didn't go down well in a, let's say, traditional village."

"I understand. When Rahim told me he liked men, I thought it was a phase, and I suggested he go to the doctor. I thought it was a symptom of his anxiety attacks," she says, embarrassed. "I feel so bad for thinking that. Honestly, I have nothing against Rahim being gay. On the contrary, I always wanted him to be happy and I didn't ask for more. I work at the Royal London Hospital Foundation. I meet a lot of gay nurses and doctors, and I have a lot of fun with them. It was while talking to them that they told me, 'Stop, Veda, Rahim is really gay! It's not anxiety.' It was a revelation. I left the hospital and went to the bank where Rahim works and hugged him to apologize and tell him that I love him just the way he is. He's the best son a mother could hope for. I felt so miserable."

Veda raises her hand to hide the shame in her eyes.

"You were perfect, Mother. I knew I could open up to you, but you were going on about stories of illness and anxiety. I didn't understand at all where you were going with that! At least I understood the confusion, and now we can laugh about it."

"I still make people laugh at the hospital with this story. This is also where I met William, who was a resident and whom I introduced to Yasmina. You see, I don't just make mistakes in life!"

"My parents are more conservative. I feel like my father wanted me to follow in his footsteps and have a family and children, because that's what he knew. And all of a sudden, it changed their perception of themselves in the eyes of their neighbors, of the village, but also in their vision of the family and the community."

"It's never easy. In our family, we're accustomed to criticism, always facing comments about our clothes, our house, our work, and our money. So, if anyone wants to comment on Rahim's orientation, they can say whatever they want, or something else, at some point..."

During the weekend, Jean-Philippe is able to chat with each member of the family. He discovers a similar passion for cycling and running with William, sports which he tries to enjoy between his work hours or when looking after Ricky. They promise to try a new mountain bike trail a few kilometers from the mansion. He speaks with Sara about his travels and even takes notes on the findings from her trip to South Africa. Above all, he answers all the questions from Yasmina who likes to investigate her big brother's lovers.

Most importantly, he spends time with Rahim who leads him to his favorite place, a wooded area behind the manor. He brings a basket with wine, bread, and cheese. On a blanket, they settle in to chat, kiss, and even make love away from prying eyes.

You don't deserve all this love. There's no point hiding your faults, they'll see them and reject you. You know that rich people don't bother with little boys like you.

17.

MOM AND COOKIES

April 2010

Jean-Philippe runs inside the airport to get to the café to join Rahim. He thinks this slow-motion race would make a great scene for a romantic movie. He can't wait any longer. He throws himself into Rahim's arms and kisses him without worrying about what the customers might think.

"What are you doing here? I can't believe you flew all this way alone! You must be sick or something?"

"I was looking at photos of you in my iPhone, and I realized I missed you terribly. I bought a plane ticket online, packed my suitcase, and got started. I know, it's crazy! But the distance was unbearable. I had to see you. It was stronger than me."

"But what about your job?"

"I made arrangements; James will be replacing me for the next few days, and we'll have five days together before I return to London. Amy drove me to the airport, and the housekeeper will take care of the apartment in my absence."

"I spoke to Amy this morning. She knew you were coming, and she didn't say anything!"

"No, I wanted it to be a surprise! But I couldn't wait for you to arrive. I was beginning to sweat, as if the airport were about to crash down on top of me, and I was being buried under a pile of debris. But enough drama. I'm happy to cuddle with you and hold you in my arms."

Rahim lifts Jean-Philippe while turning. He holds him close to erase the weeks of distance between them.

"I don't ever want us to be away for that long again," he says.

Jean-Philippe takes the suitcase and guides Rahim to the parking lot, holding his hand.

Rahim's visit fills the Genest family with joy. With his charisma and warm smile, he effortlessly endears himself to Jean-Philippe's parents. He captivates them with his natural charm, devoid of any pretentiousness. Even the queen of England wouldn't have received as much attention from them.

Marc and his son-in-law talk as if they've known each other forever. Rahim focuses his gaze on his interlocutor, as etiquette requires in his own family.

Jean-Philippe admire Rahim's exceptional qualities. He never belittles others or makes gratuitous judgments. He accepts mistakes as learning opportunities. For his part, Jean-Philippe is messy, stubborn, disorganized. It's obvious that if he compares himself, Jean-Philippe doesn't come close to Rahim.

Jean-Philippe is helping his mother clean the counter. He hears his father and his boyfriend in the distance discussing finance and sports. Rahim's presence revitalizes Marc's condition; his eyes shine, and he smiles as if the illness no longer exists.

"I'm so angry with you for keeping your boyfriend a secret from us," Michelle says. "Rahim is incredibly charming. He even took the time to give me a gift: a lovely jewelry box and a beautiful cashmere scarf."

"I love him so deeply. It's unbearable. Is this what it's like when you find the right person?" asks Jean-Philippe.

"Yes. It can be quite destabilizing, especially in the beginning."

"When I'm with him, I feel the urge to become a better person, if that makes any sense."

"Yes, I understand, and it's a challenge. You can feel like you're losing yourself, sacrificing your own identity because you prioritize the other person above all else. You risk becoming so enmeshed in the relationship that you lose sight of who you are. It's essential to realize that in love, your partner experiences the same emotions as you. He fell in love with you for your unique personality, character, and qualities. He doesn't want to lose that, and you shouldn't either."

"But I really want him to love me and not be disappointed. I never feel good enough for him."

"I may not have done much studying, but if I can teach you one thing, just one thing, it's this: a couple works by the number three."

"By three?" Jean-Philippe wonders aloud, suddenly thinking back to his evening with Samuel and Andrew.

"There's an expression that goes, 'The whole is greater than the sum of the parts.' I prefer to say, 'One plus one equals three.' It simplifies things."

"Yes, I'm familiar with the expression."

"A couple is much like that. Each person must retain their individuality, and when we come together in a relationship, they create a third entity—the couple—with its own, unique identity."

"Yes, I understand your point."

"It does require work, effort, and sacrifice. To create a strong couple, you have to be willing to contribute a part of yourself to the relationship. If we give everything without communication and merge everything, our three becomes one, and we risk losing everything. Your father had his interests, and I had mine. Together, we had our shared projects. When we respect each other's boundaries, it functions as a threesome."

"And since three is stronger than one, we must ensure that each person keeps their place, while creating a new entity, which happens to be the couple. You could write a book about it; you would be a sensation."

"Stop that. Maybe I wasn't the best mother in the world. I know we didn't make it easy for you when you were younger. I want to tell you that I wouldn't trade you for anything in the world. You were my miracle baby, and I still believe that today. I never want you to doubt it. Your boyfriend is worth it for you to build a beautiful relationship. You both possess all the qualities to make it work.”

Jean-Philippe embraces his mother tightly, sharing a deep and meaningful moment. Much like many families, Michelle had to leave school early to help support her parents. She was a beautiful woman, with brown hair, full of energy and hardworking. Working at the biscuit factory in the eastern part of Montreal, she forged friendships with people with whom she went out on weekends. She would have liked to study more, but circumstances weren’t in her favor.

She leads her life based on common sense. She doesn't claim to be perfect, but when her heart is in the right place, there's nothing that can stop her. She’s made peace with Jean-Philippe for what she has said or done in the past. No one can blame her for her lack of integrity. When she takes decisions, it's based on what she knows at that moment. If she makes a mistake, she will correct it and apologize, because it's common sense, the right thing to do.

“I couldn't have asked for a better mother. Never doubt it. Doubts are just part of my personality,” says Jean-Philippe, laughing. “Even in London, I felt your presence. I've been selfish, and I've felt a lot of anger, but I've always loved you, and that will never change.”

“What's going on in the kitchen?” shouts Marc from the living room.

“It’s none of your business,” Michelle replies. “It's a conversation between a mother and her son.”

“Then come join us in the living room.”

“I’ll finish tidying up and I'm coming.”

Jean-Philippe stands between the kitchen and the living room to listen to Marc and Rahim. The pallor of his father's sickly face has turned pink, and he gesticulates with more vigor.

"I was telling your friend that in Quebec, we watch the Montreal Canadiens games, that hockey is part of our genetic makeup."

"Be careful, Rahim, my father will try to indoctrinate you!" Jean-Philippe says, turning to Marc. "Rahim is a big sports fan too. You can talk to him about rugby, soccer, or cricket."

"I know nothing about those sports."

"That's perfect! You'll have a lot of topics to discuss in the coming days," says Jean-Philippe, smiling.

"But you never talk to me about hockey," Rahim says to Jean-Philippe.

"My relationship with hockey was rather short."

"Tell him about your first hockey experiences," Marc says.

Jean-Philippe gazes at his father with a trapped man's look. He finds no pride in sharing embarrassing stories of his youth.

"My father bought me skates to learn how to move on the ice. At first, I wasn't very good; I was young, so that was normal. In my first hockey lesson, I didn't really know what to do, so I skated around the rink instead of chasing the puck. One day, my father asked Felix to help me practice. They made me the goaler, reasoning that I wouldn't have to go far since I had to guard the net. My brother took a slap shot, just one, and the puck hit me above the eyebrow. I wasn't wearing a helmet, of course. I started bleeding profusely, and they rushed me to the emergency room for a few stitches. Now, twenty years later, the scar is still visible."

Jean-Philippe points to his right eye while Marc laughs at his son's retelling of the scar story.

Rahim stands up to get a closer look and kisses Jean-Philippe's forehead gently, as if he were a seven-year-old being consoled, resting his head against Rahim's shoulder.

Meanwhile, Jean-Philippe glances at his father, who smiles at this very normal display of affection. Marc doesn't react to this seemingly incongruous relationship, which had kept him away from his parents for so long. Have his parents changed so much in five years, or has Jean-Philippe been blind to the truth all this time?

Upon returning, Rahim asks Marc to share more stories from Jean-Philippe's childhood.

"I have plenty! You'll need many days for that," says Jean-Philippe.

"That will be another topic of conversation," adds Marc, laughing.

For three days, Jean-Philippe and Rahim literally never let go of each other's hands. Jean-Philippe introduces Rahim to Ithaca-on-the-Lake, taking him to the marina, along the river, and to his elementary school, among other places. They explore the region of his childhood, savoring the traditional poutine. They go to bed early, hoping to take advantage of the rare moments of bonding to cuddle and kiss. The presence of Jean-Philippe's parents on the upper floors keep them from indulging in more intimate activities, although... They still manage to reconnect in many other ways, lying comfortably in Jean-Philippe's small bed.

For Rahim's last dinner, Michelle is busy in the kitchen. She concocts a Bolognese sauce, which simmers all day and whose fragrance perfumes the household. Every time she prepares a pasta meal, Marc and the children enjoy it. This time, she avoids the crushed peppers to spare Marc's stomach; each guest will add them as they wish. Michelle wants a special menu for Rahim because the whole family is together, as she has so often dreamed of for several years.

Rahim, being Rahim, had packed only shirts, jackets, and chic pants in his suitcase. He puts on his nice clothes, and Jean-Philippe opts to wear his jeans. Despite the contrast, Jean-Philippe reassures Rahim about his elegance.

At Michelle's request, Jean-Philippe rearranges the room. He moves the round table and four chairs into the living room, positioning them close to Marc's bed. Michelle clears the side table next to Marc to place their meals. She plans to sit beside him, ready to assist if needed. Finally, Jean-Philippe brings the coffee table from the living room into the kitchen, along with some cushions for seating his nieces.

When they arrive, Felix's daughters kiss their grandfather. Charlie climbs onto the bed to snuggle up against him, and Marc strokes her hair while holding her against him. Meanwhile, Camille tells him about her horseback riding exploits.

Julie seats them at their table and serves them a bowl of spaghetti already cut into small pieces, accompanied by freshly baked garlic bread. The aroma of Italian cuisine puts everyone in a state of bliss. Rahim salivates, and Jean-Philippe's stomach gurgles. He helps Julie serve the plates, while Michelle sits down to cut Marc's pasta. Felix arranges the bed to ensure his father's comfort, positioning his upper body vertically. To complement the meal, Rahim uncorks two bottles of wine, a white and a red, which he purchased earlier during a shopping trip with Jean-Philippe.

"Mom, this dish is fantastic. It's so delicious," Rahim says to Michelle in English. "You're an excellent cook!"

Michelle blushes at the compliment and shyly thanks him.

"Did your boyfriend call our mother 'Mom'?" Felix asks.

"Yes, it's a tradition," Jean-Philippe replies. "I call his parents Mom and Dad too. It would be awkward to call them Stepdad or Mother-in-law... It's a mark of respect because he holds our mother in high regard. We have our biological parents and the parents we choose. But family remains family, whether it's by blood or by choice."

"Your mother didn't make this kind of meal?" Michelle asks.

"No. My mother never cooked for my two sisters and me. We had a cook at home who prepared our meals," Rahim answers candidly.

"A cook? My God, you must have been wealthy?" Felix mutters.

"Yes, Rahim's family is quite well-off, and they're wonderful people. They welcomed me as one of their own, regardless of my background or social status. I'm sorry, Mom and Dad, I don't mean anything disrespectful by that. They could see right away that Rahim and I love each other deeply, and they have complete trust in Rahim's choices."

Jean-Philippe hesitates to reveal that Rahim's family is worth billions, that every time he washes his hair, his shampoo contributes to their wealth. He would love to taunt Felix a bit, but it wouldn't accomplish anything other than making Rahim uncomfortable and causing tension. So, he keeps his inner revenge to himself. Instead, he takes Rahim's hand in his and kisses it.

Marc breaks the awkward silence.

"Rahim can call me Dad all he wants. Rahim, you are welcome to our home. When we met Julie, I immediately considered her as my daughter. It's the same for Rahim, and you should do the same, my son," Marc says to Felix.

"I'm very happy to meet you, Rahim. It was just unusual, and I was just asking a question. I hope you like it in Quebec," Felix repeats, seeking validation from his father.

"Thank you," Rahim replies like a gentleman. "I'm very happy to meet you too, and your daughters are delightful."

Jean-Philippe observes the conversation between his brother and father and has a revelation. Felix acts like Marc. He talks like him, moves like him, and imitates their father as a role model. Like Jean-Philippe, Felix has always sought validation from Marc. They just took different paths to get there. Felix followed in his father's footsteps, and Jean-Philippe did the opposite. As the black sheep of the family, he just wanted to make him react to feel like he loved him. This was how he sought his approval.

Michelle observes her entire family gathered together and smiles with great happiness. The discussions become lively, and laughter springs up. Jean-Philippe translates the conversations with difficulty between fits of laughter.

"Do you remember when Mom made us white sauce with eggs… There weren't any vol-au-vent or pastries. She served it to us like soup," says Jean-Philippe, laughing heartily and loudly.

"It's original!" says Michelle, trying to justify herself. "Vol-au-vent were expensive. So, we ate egg in white sauce, with a slice of bread to dip in it."

"Do you remember when she made us little sausages wrapped in dough?" Felix asks.

"Yes!" Jean-Philippe screams. "She baked them in the oven and then added a hot can of diced tomatoes. The dough became sticky and soft. It wasn't very good," he adds, tears in his eyes from laughter.

"What do you mean, not very good? You're telling me that now? And I thought you liked it! I made it for you often to please you," replies their mother.

"We didn't dare say anything. We were too afraid of being grounded."

They giggle. Joy and euphoria resonate in the house, a celebration forgotten for several years. Rahim doesn't understand everything but laughs as he sees them having fun. Marc restrains himself from laughing too much to avoid causing pain. The family anecdotes never end, each one funnier than the last. There is no more modesty, there are no more constraints; weeks of pressure fall away. They free themselves from repressed bitterness. To Rahim's great joy, who wants to know everything about his lover's youth, the anecdotes about his childhood begin.

"And you, Phil, who came home from Daniel's house stinking of pot. You told us all kinds of stories that made no sense! Did you really think we didn't know what you were doing?" says Michelle with a smile.

The fallen cook finally takes revenge for the teasing.

"I told myself that you didn't know what it smelled like," Jean-Philippe justifies himself.

"Your father and I let you do your experiments. We weren't born yesterday. We lived through the 1960s with peace and love and everything that that entailed!"

"So, you knew all this time that I was going to Daniel's house to drink and smoke pot?"

"We didn't really know what was going on there! But we knew you weren't very wise. I thought you'd made yourself a girlfriend. I was wrong about that, but for the rest... Did you really think that by putting your clothes in the bottom of the basket that the smell would disappear?" she confides.

Jean-Philippe looks at his mother in disbelief.

"Of course, when you arrived drunk and throwing up, it was less pleasant! I had to leave the bathroom because the noise and the smell made me feel sick."

"But you kept shouting and arguing with me!" he says.

"When I spoke, it helped me catch my breath. Don't you think Felix threw up a couple times too? He didn't give up his place. But I let your father do it; he was stronger than me in those situations."

"But you didn't say anything after that?" he says to his father.

"We should stop talking about vomit, I'm starting to feel dizzy. I didn't talk about it anymore because it's not a happy subject. You were doing your experiments, and it was fine like that, and we didn't need to talk about it over and over again. I won't start picking on you about that. We told ourselves that when you got tired of throwing up, you would stop."

Rahim stretches his arm around Jean-Philippe's shoulder while Julie and Michelle clean the table. Each week that passes in Ithaca, Jean-Philippe is rebuilding himself more and more.

He visits his room of memories, where the walls are now adorned with pictures. The trunk still spits scenes, and the floor bears the weight of time, but it feels good, perhaps even better. He confronts his most challenging memories with confidence, one at a time. Today, with dinner, Jean-Philippe can now cover a large section of the wall with his memories.

"Are you staying a few more days, Rahim?" Julie asks.

"My flight leaves tomorrow evening. I only took a long weekend to come to Quebec. I have a few meetings this week at the bank that I can't miss. I just hope the jetlag won't affect me too much," Rahim replies.

"I'll give you some tips," Jean-Philippe says kindly.

He falls asleep that evening with a light heart and joyful eyes. He lies against Rahim in his narrow bed and feels the warmth of his body, his hand pressed to his chest. He's sleeping with his lover under his parents' roof, a situation that was unthinkable a few years ago. At the time, Felix hadn't dared do so with Julie because the house rules forbade it.

The physical distance that separates Jean-Philippe and Marc allowed them to grow closer emotionally. Despite the distance that stretched between them, their bond has remained unbroken. It's a bond that has endured trials, tribulations, and challenges but has never been severed. This fact brings great comfort to Jean-Philippe.

Rahim's presence has provided Marc and Michelle with an opportunity to better understand their son. In a way, Rahim symbolizes the culmination of Jean-Philippe's life, a validation that he's making mature and responsible choices independently of his parents.

To: <u>amy.cromarty@worldcompass.com</u>

My naughty girl, you!

I thought you were loyal to me... and not to Rahim! You kept his visit to Quebec a secret from me without giving me a heads-up! But I'm just teasing you because I'm truly grateful. Your help allowed Rahim to come and join me despite his anxiety, and I know he wouldn't have done it without your support. So, thank you!

Since Rahim has been in Quebec, we've had the chance to talk. Moreover, seeing him with my parents has reminded me of the first time I met his parents. I used to focus so much on my father, but now I realize that it's my mother who has provided me with the stability and balance all these years. I was seeking validation from my father, while my mother was already giving me everything I needed, with nothing but love. It's incredible, a mother's power!

So, I've written this new mythographer, thinking of them, of all those mothers who love us unconditionally and hold their families close to their hearts.

J.P.

The Mythographers

A MOTHER'S TEARS

By Jean-Philippe Genest
Photographs by Amy Cromarty

A mother will always be a mother, whether you are one year old or thirty years old. She will worry, encourage, and reassure you. She will comfort, teach, and love you. This is what my mother tells me over and over again.

In terms of symbolism, it is rather rare that we find the words "Mom" and "Volcano" in the same sentence, except to indicate a raging anger to which only mothers have the secret. Indeed, when we think of the volcano, our mind imagines eruptions, lava flows, pyroclastic projections. With this force of nature, it is therefore normal to associate volcanoes with emotions of anger and rage. The heat of the lava and the explosions are rather far from the concept of mother, with good reason.

The volcano community

In Bolivia, within the indigenous Aymara community, volcanoes possess characteristics that differ from our typical representations. Among the Aymara people living at high altitude in the South American Andes, volcanoes are regarded as independent beings, individuals capable of movement, interaction, and even prolonged conversations. Surprising fact: the volcanoes in this region are all male, except one. This female volcano is named Tunupa. And since scarcity creates desire, the volcanoes all became enamored of Tunupa.

One day, Tunupa gave birth to a young volcano. Obviously, the bickering spread among the volcanoes, because it was impossible to know which of them was the father, since several volcanoes had courted Tunupa. The spirits of the volcanoes became heated, and battles ensued. Some went as far as to kidnap Tunupa's child to hide him in Colchani, a few kilometers to the south.

Witnesses to their altercations, the gods, disappointed and irritated by the volcanoes' behavior, took away their ability to walk and speak. Tunupa, now immobile, was devastated to be separated from her child whom she could no longer see. Every year since then, she has shed her tears and her breast milk in the valley. This mixture then creates the Uyuni salt desert at the foot of Mount Tunupa.

Salar de Uyuni

In southwest Bolivia, there is a salar, or salt desert, near the town of Uyuni. This desert is more than 10,000 km^2—three times the area of Long Island, New York or ten times the city of London. Salar de Uyuni is the largest salt desert in the world, bordered by the Tunupa volcano.

Every year, during the wet season, Salar de Uyuni is flooded both by rain and by the increasing water level of Lake Titicaca, farther north. The layer of water, by its salty character, therefore recalls the tears of Tunupa. Accumulating on the white salt, the water takes on a milky appearance. This is why the Aymara community associates the layer of water with breast milk flowing from the volcano.

Additionally, southeast of Salar de Uyuni, there is a small volcano in Colchani which also mourns the loss of its mother without knowing that they are a few kilometers from each other.

For all mothers

When I revisit the myth of Tunupa, I think of my mother, who lives thousands of kilometers from me, on another continent. A mother never forgets the true nature of her child, despite the distance, real or not, that separates her from her offspring.

Distance is an increasingly theoretical concept. The letter that took months to reach its destination is now delivered with the click of a computer. Christopher Columbus traveled ten weeks before reaching America, whereas today we change continents in less than six hours. Don't let tears invade your desert. Keep loved ones close, wherever they are in the world!

In conclusion, I have a special thought for all mothers. Wherever you are in the world, know that your child will always be connected to your heart with an indestructible thread.

The World Compass, October 2010

18.

CLOUD THE UNEXPECTED

1987

"When I say I'll wager," returned Stuart, "I mean it."

"All right," said Mr. Fogg; and, turning to the others, he continued: "I have a deposit of twenty thousand at Baring's which I will willingly risk upon it."

"Twenty thousand pounds!" cried Sullivan. "Twenty thousand pounds, which you would lose by a single accidental delay!"

"The unforeseen does not exist," quietly replied Phileas Fogg.

"But, Mr. Fogg, eighty days are only the estimate of the least possible time in which the journey can be made."

"A well-used minimum suffices for everything."

"But, in order not to exceed it, you must jump mathematically from the trains upon the steamers, and from the steamers upon the trains again."

"I will jump—mathematically."

"You are joking."

"A true Englishman doesn't joke when he is talking about so serious a thing as a wager," replied Phileas Fogg, solemnly. "I will bet twenty thousand pounds against anyone who wishes that I will make the tour of the world in eighty days or less; in nineteen hundred and twenty hours, or a hundred and fifteen thousand two hundred minutes. Do you accept?"

"We accept," replied Messrs. Stuart, Fallentin, Sullivan, Flanagan, and Ralph, after consulting each other.

"Good," said Mr. Fogg. "The train leaves for Dover at a quarter before nine. I will take it."

Despite his young age, Jean-Philippe acknowledges the considerable risks involved in this challenge. Marc estimates the current value of the bet to be around half a million dollars, making it a substantial sum riding on a perilous adventure where chance can easily change the course of events. Time is of the essence, with every moment meticulously counted, evaluated, and analyzed, and each mode of transportation must be prepared and in optimal condition. The task of predicting outcomes from billions of possibilities is a daunting one.

At the age of seven, Jean-Philippe grasps the immense risk reminiscent of Phileas Fogg's journey, yet his excitement to discover the rest of the story remains undiminished.

April 2010

Lying on Jean-Philippe's bed, his body spread out like a cross, Rahim stares at the suspended ceiling, his gaze vacant, weary. He called early to confirm his return flight only to learn seconds later that it had been canceled by the airline. By calling another airline, he discovers that all planes heading to Europe are grounded for an indefinite period. On the news channel, the reporter explains that a volcano in Iceland has erupted, with a plume of smoke and ash extending over the Atlantic and Europe. Prevailing winds carry the volcanic cloud thousands of kilometers from Iceland to Turkey. Airlines cannot risk the reactors becoming clogged with ash, endangering the lives of passengers and crew.

Rahim sees his life passing by. He unfastens his shirt collar, struggling to catch his breath. His face turns pale, and his body is overcome with cold sweat and shivers. He closes his eyes for a few moments, feeling a headache creeping in. Muffled noises surround him, and he's unable to distinguish Jean-Philippe's words.

He hates losing control over events. Rahim has planned the sequence of his day with precision since his arrival in

Quebec. His suitcase has been well organized since the day before and placed near the bedroom door, the sheets drawn tightly, the comforter folded at the foot of the bed. A sufficient number of hours are provided in case of need such as a punctured tire or an accident, multiplied by two, from which he adds the regulatory hours requested by the airline for international flights. Planning usually produces good results.

Anxiety plays tricks on Rahim and leads him into excessive imaginations. He envisions, in this apocalyptic scenario, the impossibility of returning to England while a layer of ash blankets the planet, plunging it into constant darkness and putting the population at risk of famine due to the suffocation of vegetation and the extinction of animals and humans alike.

Jean-Philippe sets out to halt the spiral that is gripping Rahim's mind. He takes Rahim's hands and compels him to make eye contact. Repeating his initial instructions several times, Jean-Philippe aims to redirect Rahim's focus toward his voice rather than his intrusive thoughts overwhelming him.

"Rahim, tell me everything that was planned for this week," he orders.

Although it reminds him of the work he's missing, Rahim must find an environment where he has control. After a few stumbles, he manages to coordinate a sentence.

"I have three meetings scheduled this week. A dinner with my mother and another with work colleagues."

"Perfect. When is the first meeting?"

"Tomorrow, 1:00 p.m."

"Excellent, you do that well. Can it be canceled or postponed?"

"No."

“All right. Can someone else do it for you?”

“Yes,” he says hesitantly. “I think James could host the meeting.”

“Perfect. You're going to call James and explain to him that you can't be there and that he has to take charge of the meeting.”

“Good idea,” Rahim says with a little enthusiasm. “I'll ask him to send me a report, and I'll follow up when I get back.”

“Fantastic. Look me in the eyes, and we’ll continue with the other meetings.”

Jean-Philippe hands him a piece of paper to write down his ideas, gradually regaining control of the situation. By traveling to Quebec, Rahim has stepped out of his comfort zone and broken down his personal barriers. He has joined Jean-Philippe in a region he doesn’t know, to meet people who didn’t even suspect his existence a few weeks ago. On a scale of one to ten of anxiety-provoking events, this trip exceeds fifteen!

“You're regaining a little color, my love. You’re breathing more easily, and you’re a lot calmer,” says Jean-Philippe to soothe him.

Still lying down, Rahim wipes his wet eyes with a handkerchief. He takes a deep breath and pulls Jean-Philippe to hug him very tightly.

“You’re my pillar, my rock,” he whispers in his lover’s ear.

“Do you realize what a feat you’ve accomplished by coming this far?”

“I needed you, and I felt that you needed me. I felt like I belonged here, with you, even if it was only for a few days. And then this damned volcano comes to screw everything up.”

"It's sending us a message. It's positive. It wants us to stay together."

They kiss tenderly while remaining entwined. Rahim has never felt the need to hold Jean-Philippe's hand as much as during this long weekend, like a thirst for resilience. Jean-Philippe doesn't complain about it.

"Rahim, I love you more than anything in the world. When you called me at the airport, I understood that you would do anything for me, and I'm ready to do anything for you too. Without saying a single word, you understand who I am, and you always respect what I want, how I feel, and you never judge me. I know I'm constantly in my head. I doubt all the time, as if I have a little demon on my shoulder who influences me negatively. You just love me, unconditionally."

"Babe, I started loving you when you stubbed out my cigarette two years ago. In that moment, I realized that you were unlike any other man, and I decided to evolve alongside you, respecting your pace, knowing that by rushing, I would risk losing you. I needed that time to adapt as well. It's easy for me to have everything I want, but living at your pace has made my desire to be closer to you grow immensely."

"Then I'll say yes," says Jean-Philippe.

"Yes, for what?"

"I'll come and live with you."

Rahim shouts with joy. They hug each other, and Rahim kisses his neck, which tickles Jean-Philippe, who laughs very hard.

"I'm starting to feel dizzy again, but I think it's the ecstasy that's making me this way."

"Hold my hand. It will always be there for you. My heart is yours, all yours. I'm ready to build our number three."

“Number three?”

“You'll have to talk to my mother,” Jean-Philippe says, laughing. “I want to invest in our relationship, and you’ll have the best of me—and the worst. I’ll still be impulsive, disorganized. I'm going to need my own moments, my own space, but I want to be close to you to build our future together.”

“I’ll always be the man who plans everything, who puts things in their place and who listens to cricket to escape and to clear my head. I want to spend the rest of my life with you, because without you, life is dreary and dull. The last few weeks have been the saddest. Previously, even if we rarely saw each other during the week, I kept smiling because the weekend was approaching. You make my life more joyful. Every day, I pinch myself to realize this isn’t a dream.”

“Me too. I feel like I'm in a dream and that I'm going to wake up without you. What a nightmare!”

Jean-Philippe and Rahim lie on the bed, face to face, eye to eye, a contact that neither of them wants to break. Rahim dives into the green eyes of his lover while Jean-Philippe adores the deep and mysterious brown of his Prince Charming.

“If you accept, I would like us to choose a new house. For both of us. I could have an office, a space of my own, and make a mess of it without feeling forced to always put it back in order.”

“That's all accepted, and for the rest, there's the cleaning lady! Babe, I'm crazy about you!”

“I've always had a reason to travel, and now I'll have a reason to come back.”

Neither wants to get out of bed. Jean-Philippe gazes at the lover he’d once dreamed of while lying in this same bed during his teenage years.

"Call James so he can take care of your meetings this week. Leave a message to your boss to explain to him that you're stuck in Quebec for a few more days. Talk to your anxiety and remind it that I'm the one in control. Do you trust me?"

"Absolutely. But I have to share something. I tried to find a flight that would go over the Pacific and Russia to get back to London," Rahim confides candidly.

Jean-Philippe observes the man of his life. His heart swells with love and happiness. Rahim opens his soul to him without restriction, without fear of judgment. He slides a hand over his lover's freshly shaved cheek.

"I believe you. In panic mode, all solutions, even the most bizarre, come to mind. Everything slips out of our hands. What you're experiencing, we've all experienced it at some point in our lives. It's like a rug being pulled out from under our feet. All I can promise you is to be your point of reference and if you lose your balance, I'll be there for you to lean on me. That reminds me of one of my favorite songs of all time, "Bridge Over Troubled Water.""

"Thank you, Babe. Do you always reference old songs?" Rahim says.

"I'm eclectic!" Jean-Philippe replies with enthusiasm. "I'm going to go tell my parents that you're finally staying for a few more days. They're going to be really happy about this. They love you very much."

"I love them too."

Rahim takes off his sweat-dampened shirt and, having no clean clothes at hand, he puts on jeans and a t-shirt from Jean-Philippe's dresser. He sits in the living room with his boyfriend and his in-laws, feeling awkward in these unfamiliar clothes, but he lets go, embracing his newfound mindset.

"Has a plane ever tried to fly through a volcanic cloud?" Michelle asks.

"From what I recall, this happened at least twice in the 1980s. In Indonesia, a British Airways Boeing flew over a volcano, and all four engines stopped. This also happened with a KLM flight in Alaska. The ash blocked the turbines, and the pilot was only able to restart them once the residue had blown away with the force of the wind. A stroke of luck."

"How do you manage to know so much about so many things?" Marc asks.

"I had a good model! You remember all the questions I asked when I was young. I felt like you knew everything, and I wanted to be like you. It's easy when you have the interest," replies Jean-Philippe.

Placing his hand on Jean-Philippe's thigh, Rahim adds, "I'm fascinated by his ability to remember everything. I love listening to him recount travel stories and share anecdotes about Amy. He has a knack of explaining things in a simple yet captivating manner."

Jean-Philippe looks at him and winks.

"Since it's current, do you happen to know the story of the troll of Eyjafjallajökull, the volcano with the unpronounceable name?" asks Jean-Philippe, attempting a rough Icelandic accent.

"No, and I've never heard of the volcano either," says Marc.

Jean-Philippe stands up to narrate the legend, mimicking the voices and reenacting the gestures of the characters.

"For centuries, deep within the heart of the volcano, dwelled the notorious troll Gilitrutt, renowned for trapping humans. Such was the nature of trolls worldwide. Now, an Icelandic farmer had wed a young woman in hopes that she would assist in his farm work. He assigned her the task of weaving the wool from his sheep. However, she proved to be lazy, always putting her work off to the following day. One fateful day, a gigantic woman appeared at the farmer's doorstep, offering to undertake the weaving on her behalf. When the farmer's wife inquired about the cost, the portly woman proposed an exchange: if she could guess her first name within three attempts, the job would be free. The young wife, considering it a stroke of luck, eagerly accepted the proposition.

"Afterward, the farmer's wife, who was not particularly astute, realized the immense challenge of guessing the woman's first name with no clue whatsoever. She confessed everything to her husband, who informed her that the woman was far from ordinary; she was a troll who would abduct her if she failed to solve the riddle.

"A few weeks later, while ascending Eyjafjallajökull, the farmer stumbled upon the troll's cave and overheard her humming: 'Ho! Ho! She doesn't know my first name. Hey! Hey! Gilitrutt is my name.'

"Upon his return, he decided to teach a valuable lesson to his wife and made her wait until summer. Eventually, out of compassion for his increasingly anxious spouse, he revealed the troll's first name to her. When Gilitrutt returned with the woven wool, the giantess was astonished that the farmer's wife knew the answer and hastily retreated to the mountaintop, never to be seen again. Fear transformed the farmer's wife into a committed and organized woman, who thereafter worked diligently on weaving wool without anyone's help."

"And is it because of this troll that the volcano erupts as it does?" Marc inquires.

"In part," Jean-Philippe responds. "Since Gilitrutt can no longer weave, she has chosen to disrupt people's lives in a different manner. It compels us to slow down and reflect. Are the shortcuts we take really worth it, and are we prepared to face the consequences, whatever they may be? Are we ready to confront our inner trolls when they come to collect their dues? For we all have many trolls, concealed at the recesses of a trunk, a drawer, or in the depths of our minds."

Jean-Philippe returns to his seat beside Rahim. In truth, the moral of the story was directed at him personally. The entity that Jean-Philippe must confront resides within himself. He must embark on weaving his own personal woolen thread, a task that no one else can undertake on his behalf.

"Rahim, tomorrow I'm taking you to visit Montreal. We'll explore Mount Royal, Saint Joseph's Oratory, the Old Port. After this emotionally charged long weekend, I'd like to show you a piece of my home to take to our home in London. We'll take the opportunity to enjoy a beaver tail."

"A beaver tail?" Rahim frowned. "I'm not familiar with that."

"It's a type of pastry."

"Well, you're the expert on that subject, and I'm certainly up for it if it doesn't bother you, Mom and Dad?" Rahim asks.

"Have a great time! You're young, and there's a lot of
life ahead of you. Don't wait for a volcano to disrupt your
living. Find the positives in challenges," Marc advises him.

19.

SHOCKWAVE EFFECTS

August 2005

Sainte Catherine Street, in the center of the Gay Village, comes alive with a vibrant and colorful atmosphere. All the shops and restaurants display the colors of the rainbow flag. The festivities surrounding Pride Week offer numerous activities, another opportunity for Jean-Philippe and his friends to celebrate. Along with Jake and Mathieu, he frequents the bars to have a drink or two—or more—and move his hips on the dance floors, even if Jean-Philippe isn't the best dancer in town.

Each day has a theme linked to personalities who have led important battles for the LGBT community in Quebec and around the world. This year is particularly festive, with the recognition of same-sex marriage in Canada. Shows in parks and street performers entertain passers-by. Men kiss each other, elderly ladies leer at the dancers with bare buttocks waddling to the techno music that punctuates their steps. There is no embarrassment; the Village is a safe and free space in these times of celebration.

Jake and Mathieu, two athletes who are part of the gay swimming team, try to convince Jean-Philippe to join them in parading on their allegorical float.

"Come on! It's Sunday, the last day of festivities. We're going to have fun! In the afternoon, it will be over, and there will be lots of handsome guys! Afterward, we're going to stay and dance in the street!" argues Mathieu.

"You'll be with your whole swimming team. Are you sure?" Jean-Philippe asks.

"Stop that nonsense. You're perfect. The more people, the better. We're all going to have the same costume. It's going to be decorated, and we're going to accompany two drag queens. It's going to be sick!"

"Won't I look crazy? You all have broad shoulders, and I'm all thighs."

"I'm sure! It's fun when there are a lot of people on the float. We don't care if you're a swimmer or not. Everyone will drool over your pecs and your butt. And the rest of us will dance and won't care about the rest."

"Perfect, I'm on board. You'll tell me where I should meet you, and at what time!"

The multi-colored balloons, the gold and silver garlands, as well as the fake plastic palm trees brighten up the allegorical float draped with a large red carpet, eagerly awaiting the dancers. Team posters encircle the tank at the wheel level.

Jean-Philippe, shirtless like all the swimmers in the tank, dons tight-fitting, metallic blue shorts and white sneakers. His task is simple: dance to the music blasting from the enormous speakers. Jake adds two black lines under Jean-Philippe's eyes like a football player, emphasizing his athletic physique. He ties two blue ribbons to his biceps to maintain a consistent look among the participants, showcasing his new tattoo on his arm and shoulder.

All through the day, the friends toss paper hearts into the crowd. The spectators dance to the music, and the athletes greet the spectators with confetti swirling in the wind. Jean-Philippe has never felt more accepted than when he sees the thousands of people lining the boulevard. The city's warmth permeates their hearts.

They move around the street all afternoon, fueled by Red Bulls, until the early hours of the morning. Jean-Philippe has stopped counting the number of beers and shots offered to him, as well as the number of men he has greedily kissed.

Waking up on Monday morning is pretty rough—hangover, messy and sticky hair, partial memory. Fragments of his brain are certainly still lying around the Village. The muscles in his legs beg him to stay in bed, and he struggles to get to the bathroom. Jean-Philippe doesn't remember ever dancing so much in a single day. He recalls certain men he met during the evening. His tight blue shorts caught the attention of more than one, as did his phoenix tattoo, which he proudly displayed. The bird's feathers wrap around his bicep, and its wings extend across its chest, with the fanciful tail reaching down to the elbow. How many men allowed themselves to touch his chest under the pretext of caressing the mythical beast? After all, wasn't that the reason for choosing a tattoo on this body part? Jean-Philippe trains to please, and it works. He's not going to complain.

He relaxes before breakfast. He grabs the sole brown-speckled banana on the counter and a bowl of Rice Krispies. He showers under a jet of invigorating hot water to ease his shoulders. While drying off, he hears the postman putting the mail in the mailbox. In boxers, he goes out to collect it and put the various advertisements into the recycling bin. He keeps in his hand the long-awaited letter from London, bearing the *World Compass* logo in the upper left corner.

Jean-Philippe applied to join a team of young reporters at the famous magazine. The contract, lasting one year, allows novices to accompany experienced journalists as they travel the planet.

He sent his contact details, his experiences, as well as two examples of articles in English he has already published. He subsequently gave a telephone interview. Since then, he has been impatiently awaiting the answer.

You have trouble getting hired in Montreal. Do you honestly think a London magazine will hire you? Let's be realistic about your dreams!

With trembling hands, he tears open the envelope. He unfolds the letter and reads the sentences several times before sitting down on the ground, his legs giving way. He lies on the kitchen floor, exhaling in euphoria. The magazine has hired him as a paid intern, one of five junior reporters selected to work at *World Compass* for a year.

Ecstasy takes over his body and he wakes up his roommate to share the good news. He asks him for his car to go to his parents and finally prove his worth to them. At last, he's crossing a new stage in his life; news of his success will travel around Ithaca-on-the-Lake faster than a football championship. The smile never leaves his face. On August 15th, 2005, *Around the World in Eighty Days* is no longer just a book for Jean-Philippe, but a reality.

Jean-Philippe arrives at his parents' house in the middle of the afternoon. He parks the old Tercel in the street in front of the house and gets out, holding the acceptance letter in his hand like a trophy. He quickly climbs the steps two by two like a child. He knocks but enters without waiting.

"My God, you scared me!" exclaims Michelle.

"It's just me! Sorry to have surprised you," he says.

He laughs and speaks loudly, but his parents react minimally. He kisses Michelle on the cheek, and she returns the gesture coldly. The atmosphere in the house is as icy as a day in February. Seated at the table, his father glares at him and doesn't even offer him a hello.

"Are you okay?" Jean-Philippe asks shyly. "Did something happen? Somebody died?"

No one answers, and the mystery becomes uncomfortable. Jean-Philippe cannot understand their reaction. Marc and Michelle look at each other in silence.

"Is there anything I can do?" he asks. "You'll have to tell me what's wrong if you want me to help you."

"It's a good thing you're here. I'll be able to ask you my questions directly. I would like you to answer me honestly," replies Marc. "As honestly as possible."

What have you done again?

"Of course. No problem with that." Although perplexed, Jean-Philippe speaks calmly as he remains standing beside the kitchen table.

"How do you consider your mother and me?"

"What do you mean by 'consider'? You're my parents. My father, my mother. I owe you my life!" he quips to lighten the atmosphere.

"Stop acting innocent and answer the question. What do you think of your father and mother?"

"Well, I don't know what to answer. Actually, I don't know what you want me to answer. I don't know why you're asking me these questions. You're my parents. Normal parents, who have normal lives, with normal children. You are… normal! Is this the answer you want?"

"Do you think we're normal? You don't think we're backward? Behind the times?"

"No, I don't think that! Who told you things like that?"

"It's you, big doofus! And 'backward' is exactly the word you used!"

"But where does this nonsense come from?"

"From this morning's newspaper!" Marc points to the newspaper folded on the table.

"There's a report on yesterday's gay parade in Montreal, with lots of beautiful color photos. Who do we see in the newspaper? Our tall, innocent son in underwear, shirtless with a tattoo on his arm and flowers on his neck," he sarcastically jokes. "But the most incredible thing is what is written below the picture! Wait, I'll read the excerpt to you."

Marc grabs the newspaper and folds it to hold it more firmly. His tone of voice carries a mixture of anger and disappointment.

"The journalist asks: 'Why do you think it's important to hold a parade as part of Montreal Pride Week?' A young man named Jean-Philippe Genest responds, 'The parade is an important event because it expresses to Quebecers and the whole world that the fight isn't over. We've taken a step forward with the legalization of gay marriage, but there's still much to do. I come from a small village where homosexuality isn't yet accepted. Mentalities are a bit backward, and we need to move ideas forward so that everyone feels safe in their bodies and in their lives. Coming out was difficult for me, and I hope that the future offers greater openness to all young people.' "

Jean-Philippe remains silent, speechless, stunned. Michelle leans against the counter, arms crossed, and Marc throws the newspaper on the table, looking at his son in silence.

Well done, champion. Another thing you don't remember from last night!

"That's what you think of your parents! That we're backward? That we gave you trouble with your homosexuality?" probes Marc.

"I wasn't talking about you in particular. It was more in general. I mean, that's what many people in the region experience. You can't say that you accepted my homosexuality with the greatest enthusiasm," Jean-Philippe justifies himself.

"Because we should have been happy too! You didn't tell us that. Our son is gay! Let's celebrate!" his father says sarcastically.

"Well, no, but it doesn't matter! We won't come back to that. It's in the past."

Marc approaches his son, so close that Jean-Philippe can see the blood pulsating below his father's eyes.

"What's even more insulting is that you talk about the village, our neighbors, as if they were backward! I am mayor of this town, doing my best to make it a pleasant place. But what were you thinking? We provided you with everything. We paid for your education. You went to Montreal for college and university to make things easier. We sacrificed for all those years, and the first thing we hear is that our big doofus thinks we're not good enough for him. You drink, you go out, you get tattoos, all while your parents work hard in the background. But none of that matters because they're supposedly backward! They come from a place filled with people who aren't up to the standards of Montreal!"

"You're exaggerating! That's not at all what's written."

Jean-Philippe folds the letter he had in his hand, puts it back in his pocket, and takes a step away to reduce the tension in the kitchen.

"And now I'm exaggerating too! I'm not smart enough to understand what's written in a newspaper. The big doofus is going to have to explain that to us because we're not bright enough to understand," Marc says, turning to Michelle and then Jean-Philippe. "You think you're smarter than the rest of us! You come see us when it suits you. You have no consideration. You're just heartless. But it doesn't matter, they won't understand anyway. You'll be able to manipulate us as you want," he says indignantly.

"That's not what I think at all," Jean-Philippe says. "It's true that you had difficulty with my coming out. If I remember your words correctly, you said, 'I hope you won't become effeminate!' Do you remember that, Mom? You were so afraid of what the village was going to say, of the gossip that the neighbors were going to spread, that my appearance was going to create a panic. All of a sudden, it upset Mr. and Mrs. So-and-so. Your boy is tired of hiding. I spent my entire adolescence lying so no one would be disgusted, so that you wouldn't suffer the consequences. I'd suspected it for a long time and said nothing. Why do you think I came out at twenty-three? Twenty-three years old, do you realize that it's late? Your Phil has come out of the closet, and he has no intention of going back in.

"I'm happy, and I have friends with whom I can confide, people I trust who listen to me and who hear me. I am who I am, and you'll have to get used to it. If I feel like dressing like a woman, I don't see why that would concern you, and if I have a boyfriend who is effeminate, well, that's none of your business either. I won't hide anymore; those days are over. At some point, someone has to tell you, and if it took the newspaper to realize that I exist despite my differences, it will at least have served that purpose."

Suddenly, Marc's large hand rises and slaps Jean-Philippe's cheek. The force of the blow sends his head over his shoulder, knocking him off balance. Strong heat rises in his face, intense pain invading his skin. The sound of the slap rings in his ears. He no longer hears anything else; all the noises in the house are muffled as if in the depths of a cave. Jean-Philippe puts his hand on his cheek, his mouth open, and looks at Marc in amazement.

"Marc, don't!" Michelle shouts.

She intervenes between the two to prevent Jean-Philippe from responding. It's useless. The rule of non- violence is at the heart of the Genests' education and values but today, it has been broken by the very man who established it. Never, ever, has Marc raised his hand against anyone, and Jean-Philippe respected this rule to the letter, the only one he truly followed. The Genests screamed, they cried, but they always found a solution other than violence.

"To hit someone is to take away their dignity."

Tears well, but Jean-Philippe doesn't cry. Rage invades his heart and lungs. He wants to scream out all the pain he feels at this precise moment, but a knot forms, preventing him from breathing. His hand trembles, and he slips it into his pocket to take out the folded letter. He throws it on the table and says, "You will never see my face here again."

Jean-Philippe turns his back and walks toward the door with a resolute step. He closes the door gently—because it's forbidden to slam doors—and grabs the banister to go down the few steps. His legs falter. Nevertheless, he stands tall and proud to walk to the car. He opens the door, sits in, and drives off. He wipes his eyes with the sleeves of his plaid shirt. He drives and stops the car at the side of the empty road a kilometer farther along the way. He begins to scream, a cry that rends the soul. He screams until the lump in his throat disappears.

Today he has lost two people: his father and his hero.

A month passes, and Jean-Philippe prepares his luggage for London. His roommates and friends organize a farewell party. He leaves serenely toward an adventure he has dreamed of since his childhood. Temporary accommodations await him very close to the *World Compass* offices where he must report by October 1st.

The phone vibrates and displays a call from Ithaca-on-the-Lake, but Jean-Philippe declines.

"Well, when do we begin to drink?" he asks his friends.

They all grab beers straight from the fridge. The discussions become lively, and "Space Oddity" by David Bowie is played to forget the troubles of the past and celebrate the future. Like he can hear in the lyrics, he's ready to leave his capsule, floating above the ground.

Let's begin the countdown and ignite the engines.

20.

AGAINST ALL ODDS

April 2010

The episodes of pain come more frequently, and Marc finds it increasingly challenging to tolerate the medication. Moments of clarity are spaced out over time. Despite the hardships, he refuses to pity himself and accepts his fate with dignity.

Jean-Philippe helps Michelle with daily tasks and keeps Marc company. Rahim flew back to London six days later when the Icelandic volcano calmed down and flights resumed. Although catastrophic, the eruption united the lovers, allowing them an impromptu reconnection. They took advantage of these days off to begin their search for a new home. Among their criteria, Jean-Philippe wants a more rustic architecture while Rahim prefers a more modern style. Since Rahim's departure,

Jean-Philippe has given himself a new routine: he texts Rahim every morning so as to never lose contact with him again. He has started running again to give himself some energy, as the days were becoming more and more exhausting.

He misses traveling as well as contact with Amy. She writes to her friend often to support him morally by sending him words of encouragement, or simply photos of men she finds handsome. She's beginning preparations for their next assignment. She leaves it to Jean-Philippe to decide between Sri Lanka or Madagascar, two destinations he dreams of visiting. "You don't make it easy for me," he writes to her.

Jean-Philippe adjusts Marc's pillow while he absently watches television.

His father turns to him to speak. "I really like Rahim."

"Me too," says Jean-Philippe, smiling.

"He's a charming boy, and I'm glad you two get along well. When I look at you, I see myself again on my first dates with Michelle. I wish you to be happy for a very long time. You deserve it," Marc says, his eyes moist.

Jean-Philippe smiles to indicate that he hopes just as much.

"I know it's hard to put into words, but I feel really good with Rahim. When we look into each other's eyes, it's like we understand everything. I have the feeling that he understands what's going on in my head," he says.

"That's chemistry. It's something you have to experience. It can't be explained."

"That must be it."

"I know that marriages between men are now legal. I wish you with all my heart to experience it one day. I don't know about England, but otherwise you could do it here," says Marc.

"The UK doesn't recognize gay marriage yet. Maybe someday. We'll take one day at a time and see where it takes us. I'm not closing the door on the idea. We'll have to wait and see."

"He'll say yes, if you ask him," he says with a wink.

"I see that you haven't only spoken of my bad childhood antics."

Marc smiles, a softness in his eyes.

"You know, in the last few weeks, I've had the chance to reflect on my life, on the happy moments with Michelle, with Felix, with the girls, and with you too," he confides.

Jean-Philippe approaches the bed and sits down. He takes his father's hand in his.

"The last five years have been difficult, very difficult. I no longer had my Phil to talk to. You know it always made me feel good when you came back from Montreal. You always had a lot to say. You know how to tell stories so well. It was always funnier every time. When your mother arrived, and you repeated the anecdotes by changing the story a little, I laughed because I knew you'd changed the story. It was subtle and clever. You know how to handle words with finesse."

Marc catches his breath and coughs a little before returning to his confidences. "I missed it terribly. I felt like I was failing as a father, and it killed me. For five years, I've been dying slowly, like your old volcanoes. I know I was hard on you. I know I hurt you and crossed the line. I want to apologize for hitting you. It's inexcusable, but I apologize anyway."

Jean-Philippe rubs his father's hand with his thumb to reassure him. He leans his head on his father's hand to kiss it.

He remains in this position for several minutes, crying. With his other hand, Marc caresses his son's hair with tenderness. Jean-Philippe had been waiting for this moment for so long.

"This cancer, it's like all the guilt that's been building up inside me, eating away at my body from within. I look at you today, I see a man I'm proud of. You're beautiful inside and out. You live your life with honor, kindness, and generosity. I'm happy with the person you've become, but sometimes I wonder if I truly deserve to be your father."

His clouded eyes reveal the remorse that is devouring Marc from the inside. Jean-Philippe's father offers him his most sincere apologies. For one last time, he wishes to play his role as father for all the failings of the last five years.

"Don't say that, Dad. You're my hero, and you always will be. I wouldn't be the man I am if I hadn't had you as a role model. I was so fortunate! Every evening, my father would spend time talking with me before bedtime. None of my friends had that kind of connection with their dad. It was such precious time for me. I didn't care about Christmas presents or my birthday. All I wanted was moments with you. I used to ask for books just so you could read them to me. You knew everything. I must have asked you a million questions, but you never got angry, and you never lost patience. You always had an answer, and if not, you'd find it in the encyclopedias. You were my Phileas Fogg. You took me on journeys. You protected me from the bad guys as best you could. You let me live in my own world and, most importantly, you let me dream."

"I always knew you wouldn't have an ordinary life. When you were little, do you remember building a village with the Tupperware containers you took out of the cupboards? If only you knew how much I wanted to follow you in your dreams. I lived my dreams through yours. You were free as the air, floating like a feather in the wind. Was I jealous? A little... But instead of holding you back, as I did, I should have let you go. In the end, you left without me. And without you, I lost my bearings. My Phil had disappeared.

"Your mother was angry with me for a long time for breaking up the family. I knew she was calling you in London. She did it secretly, but she didn't hide very well. At the beginning, I had my pride. I thought you'd call to apologize. Today, I know you didn't have to do it. It's my fault you left, and Michelle was right to be mad at me. I was selfish and cared too much about what people thought. Now I realize it! We don't care so much about their opinions. I put others before you and that's where I lost you. That's where I lost myself."

"I shouldn't have spoken to you the way I did. It was completely inappropriate. It's not all your fault. I have my share of responsibility in this, and I blame myself too. There hasn't been a day that I haven't thought of you two. I have my stubbornness too. We know who I got that from," Jean-Philippe adds to make him smile. "I also apologize for all the worries I put you through, for everything I said."

"You don't need to apologize for standing up for yourself. I had a young man in front of me who wasn't afraid to express himself, who was proud and who took responsibility. Today, I have before me a man whom I wouldn't trade for all the gold in the world."

Marc asks for some water to drink. Jean-Philippe puts a straw in the glass before giving it to him.

"I would like to ask you to take care of your mother when I'm gone."

"Yes, I will," replies Jean-Philippe earnestly. "But with her here and me in London, it might be complicated. There's a great distance that separates us."

"You know, my boy, distance isn't measured in kilometers but in the absence of human contact."

"You're philosophizing now!"

"You can be on the other side of the village or in the same house and never worry about your mother. You can be on another continent and still feel close to her. Contact is two beings touching each other, but who says it has to be skin to skin?"

"Yes, that's true."

"That's all I ask of you. I want you to live your life the way you choose it. Without compromise, like the man I have in front of me. Promise me that you won't bow to anyone. Never."

"I promise you. I will be a man, like you."

After all these emotions, Marc grows tired quickly and closes his eyes to doze off. Jean-Philippe turns up the volume on the television to help him sleep. He'll engrave each of these words in his memory so that they'll live forever, even after his father is gone.

21.

TEMPUS FUGIT

1989

How was it that a man so exact and fastidious could have made this error of a day? How came he to think that he had arrived in London on Saturday, the twenty-first day of December, when it was really Friday, the twentieth, the seventy-ninth day only from his departure?

The cause of the error is very simple.

Phileas Fogg had, without suspecting it, gained one day on his journey, and this merely because he had travelled constantly eastward; he would, on the contrary, have lost a day had he gone in the opposite direction, that is, westward.

In journeying eastward he had gone towards the sun, and the days therefore diminished for him as many times four minutes as he crossed degrees in this direction. There are three hundred and sixty degrees on the circumference of the earth; and these three hundred and sixty degrees, multiplied by four minutes, gives precisely twenty-four hours—that is, the day unconsciously gained. In other words, while Phileas Fogg, going eastward, saw the sun pass the meridian *eighty* times, his friends in London only saw it pass the meridian *seventy-nine* times. This is why they awaited him at the Reform Club on Saturday, and not Sunday, as Mr. Fogg thought.

"So, Phileas Fogg lived a day more than his friends in London?" asks Jean-Philippe.

"In theory, that's correct. It didn't show because he was traveling very slowly going east. Every day the sun set a little earlier. He gained a few minutes every day. In total for his trip, he managed to accumulate all these minutes to recover an entire day."

"It's difficult to understand!"

"I know. These days, we talk about jet lag. For example, it's currently evening here and in France, it's already early morning. We could take a flight that leaves at noon from

Montreal and arrive in Vancouver three hours later, and still be noon!”

“Wow! That’s completely crazy! But at least it was a mistake that made Phileas Fogg win.”

His father opens the atlas to illustrate the division of the earth into different time zones and teaches him how to calculate times, thus helping him avoid time errors when traveling.

“Since the sun illuminates one side of the earth at a time, it cannot be midday everywhere. As it turns on its axis—a process known as rotation—each complete revolution represents a day. Time passes as the earth rotates, with people on one side going about their day while others sleep.”

Marc points out the date line and explains to his son that by crossing this line, the date changes. Phileas Fogg was supposed to move his time back a day, but he forgot to change the date. It's as if he could travel through time, going back a day to experience it all over again.

May 2010

Yesterday, Marc died. He left his world peacefully, surrounded by Michelle, the love of his life, and his two sons.

According to his wishes, he’d received Julie and his two granddaughters the previous week. They brought a drawing of birds with hearts inscribed with words of love. Felix posted it on the living room wall opposite his bed. Marc would have liked to see them grow up longer, but he promised Felix and Julie that he would watch over them in the afterlife. He believed in the world of spirits, and Michelle felt reassured to know he would be there. Skeptical, Jean-Philippe doubts this post-mortem existence, even though he's the greatest defender of giants, trolls, dragons, and witches. It's a bit paradoxical, but it's how he is.

To make his father smile, Jean-Philippe told him, "I don't want you to scare me. I forbid you from appearing to me like a ghost. And if you're mad at me, find another way to tell me!"

Uncles, aunts, and friends came to visit Marc in the last weeks. Everyone took a moment to talk while he still had the strength. He took his last breath while Michelle held his hand. He flew away, with peace of mind, accompanied by all the love of his family.

Jean-Philippe wakes up early, as usual, and dons stretchy pants and his sneakers. He slips on a t-shirt and his spring coat since, on this May morning, the temperature remains cool. He ascends from his room and crosses the vacant living room. Stepping out onto the balcony, he begins his warm-up. He stretches the muscles of his thighs and calves, concluding with a rotation of the ankles.

He inserts small earphones, heads toward the church, and then runs along the main street. The village is just waking up, and a few birds are chirping happily. Spring is slowly transitioning into summer, with leaves turning green on the tree branches. He climbs the railroad embankment and halts in front of the railroad tracks. Jean-Philippe places his foot on the rail and walks like a tightrope walker on the steel beam. He continues his journey in balance, then leaps from one wooden crossing to another, covering several meters while listening to "Father and Son" by Cat Stevens, the lyrics of the song capturing the essence of his relationship with his father.

The railway line cuts the village in two, serving as a border that separates two territories. It's a boundary without much thickness, easily crossed with a simple stride. Jean-Philippe walks along this border, a theoretical line dividing two distinct areas. On one side, there's the old district, clustered around the church and town hall, and on the other, a more modern landscape with its bungalows and parks. One side embodies tradition, while the other represents a newer expanse. He ambles along this boundary, unsure of which direction to choose.

You're going to get hit! You're pathetic for always hesitating between the past and the future. Get with the program! Are you staying here or are you going back to London? With Rahim, without Rahim, in his condo, in your apartment... You suck! You'll never be able to resume your life without your father. You had someone to hate, and now he's gone. How will you manage?

There are so many words that have remained unspoken. Words that reverberate in Jean-Philippe's mind like a fanfare. A thunderous noise that drowns all other sounds. A saboteur who clamors louder, attempting to smother the flame of reason. It's time to confront this adversary because his true nemesis was never his father; it is something else.

Jean-Philippe takes a long breath, gazes up at the sky, and then focuses on the two railroad tracks converging on the horizon.

"Dear saboteur, the one who judges, the one who controls, the one who avoids. Thank you for wanting to protect me. You have been a constant presence in my life, always trying to be kind, but in reality, your influence has often been discouraging. I am Phileas Fogg, and I yearn for adventures. I want to share my life with Rahim and embark on the most beautiful love story, because I truly believe I deserve it. Therefore, I'm bidding you farewell.

"Yes, from this moment forward, I will only lend an ear to your voice if it carries a positive message. I'm leaving you here, at the railway line, on the border that separates my past and my future. I want you to understand that life isn't a straight path; it's a journey where each destination marks the beginning of a new adventure. Ithaca-on-the-Lake is my point of origin, a piece of me that I will carry with me wherever I go and plant in my new home. The future remains unknown, just as it does for you.

"I'm a reflection of my father and mother, I'm Ithaca, I'm Montreal and Quebec. I'm London, Rahim, Amy, a journalist, a geographer, and I'm proudly gay. I'm the culmination of my relationships, experiences, and the territories I walk on. I exist because of who I have been and who I will become. I'm the world, boundless and borderless.

"Dear saboteur, I thank you for your past services. However, starting now, I'm embracing risk. I'm reclaiming control over my life and my destiny."

Jean-Philippe resumes jogging again through the village streets, heading in different directions—south, northeast, and west—without a specific destination in mind, simply running for the sake and joy of it.

Amy accompanies Rahim to Marc's funeral. Earlier in the week, they took a flight to Montreal to join Jean-Philippe. The small wooden church quickly fills with townspeople who have gathered to bid farewell to their mayor. As the church becomes crowded, the residents spill over into the organ gallery area, and some are left standing behind the nave and along the walls. The bishop of the diocese presides over the ceremony, and the local member of the National Assembly of Quebec pays tribute to his friend during the service.

Michelle and her family occupy the first rows before the coffin arrives. Michelle is dressed in a black skirt and jacket paired with a white blouse, signifying sobriety and tastefulness. Rahim, who always has a sense of style with his new Tom Ford black wool-suit, assisted Jean-Philippe in selecting an outfit for the occasion. He chose a charcoal gray suit along with a matching shirt, allowing him to forgo wearing a tie. Camille and Charlie are dressed in adorable little blue dresses adorned with burgundy bows, adding a touch of color to this somber day, as per Marc's wishes.

The village council has reserved the community room adjoining the town hall to receive guests after the burial at the cemetery. The family gathers to receive kind words, and even the prime minister of Quebec has sent a letter through the MP. Marc's generosity and kindness are repeatedly mentioned—people speak of him as a truly good-hearted gentleman.

Condolences are offered to Michelle, Felix, and Julie, concluding with Jean-Philippe and his partner.

Rahim charms everyone, even those who don't understand English. Marc had often talked about his son, the globe-trotting journalist based in England. For many neighbors and friends, meeting Jean-Philippe feels like a reunion. Other citizens eagerly rush to greet Marc's son, and at that moment, Jean-Philippe realizes that stories about him have circulated throughout the village more than once. He wipes away a tear from his cheek, and Rahim places a supportive hand on his back.

Daniel, Jean-Philippe's childhood friend, arrives to meet him, accompanied by his wife Laura, who happens to be the first and only woman Jean-Philippe has ever kissed. They engage in quiet conversation, catching up on the time they've missed while sharing photos of their two-year-old son. Laura reveals that she's expecting their second child at the end of the year. The couple expresses their desire for Jean-Philippe to become the godfather of their unborn baby. They make a promise to meet again before returning to London and to stay in touch thereafter.

After the reception, Amy drives to Jean-Philippe's childhood home in her rented Jeep. Jean-Philippe gazes at the familiar surroundings, his two most important companions by his side. Amy mentions that she would have traveled anywhere in the world to be there for her friend, emphasizing the strength of their bond. Rahim leans forward from the back seat, eager to listen to what Jean-Philippe and Amy have to share.

"It was a beautiful ceremony," Amy says.

"I believe it too. My mother is very satisfied," Jean-Philippe replies pragmatically.

"And you look very handsome in your suit," Rahim adds, placing his hand on Jean-Philippe's shoulder.

"I look at the house and think of my father. I spent my entire childhood in that house, and I moved away from them believing I wasn't loved, that I wasn't good enough, not kind enough, not smart enough. I wasted five years of my life out of pride, out of resentment. I blame myself so much," Jean-Philippe confesses.

"Your father wasn't perfect, but he was there," Rahim says. "Mine worked all the time. We have a great relationship, but he doesn't really know me. It's easy not to make mistakes when you're not present."

Jean-Philippe reflects, "All I dream of today is having one more day with my father. Just one. I want to tell him that I love him. I want to tell him that he was my hero and always has been. I would like to do like Phileas Fogg, discover an anomaly in space-time, and gain an extra day."

"What did your father say? It's not the distance that matters, it's the contact, or something like that," Rahim recalls. "You may have wasted five years because you both had misplaced pride, but in recent months, you were reunited with the father you lost. Now you have to mourn a man who is no longer here physically, but you won't have regrets, because he'll live in you forever," he adds sympathetically.

The man in his life consistently offers words of wisdom that provide comfort. Rahim's insight resonates deeply because it reminds him that his father's presence will endure, regardless of his location on the planet. He can now fulfill his promise to take his father on a journey, as his father will always be there with him, accompanying him on his adventures.

The house regains its familiar appearance, and the living room returns to its former state. Felix has returned the adjustable bed, the wheel chair, and the furniture is back to its original places. Michelle kindly offered Amy the use of her bed and room during her stay in Quebec, but Amy declined and insisted on sleeping on the couch. She finds it surprisingly comfortable, even more so than in many places she has slept around the world.

Michelle and Amy's friendship grows during this time, and they share the preparation of meals together. Michelle frequently repeats how much Marc would have adored Amy. Marc had a deep appreciation for individuals of integrity and authenticity, qualities that Amy possesses. These qualities also contribute to Rahim's undeniable charm.

As the friends converse in the kitchen, Michelle brings a box over to Jean-Philippe.

"This is for you. Your father wanted me to give it to you after the funeral," she says to her son.

Curious, Jean-Philippe inquires, "What is this?"

"It's up to you to discover. I'm heading to bed. I'll give you a kiss and wish you a good night. I believe I'll sleep well tonight. Don't forget to turn off the lights before going to bed."

Michelle blows Jean-Philippe a kiss and winks before heading upstairs. Jean-Philippe cradles the box in his hands, treating it like a precious and fragile treasure. It's a simple cardboard box with worn corners, devoid of any labeling or indication. Slightly larger than a shoebox, it could have held a hat or any other object of similar size.

Amy watches with eager anticipation, her impatience showing in her expression. "Open it! What are you waiting for?"

He carefully lifts the lid and uncovers the last five years of his life neatly arranged inside. Wrapped in a ribbon, he finds all the postcards he has sent to his mother. Every single one is there: Paris, Buenos Aires, Cairo, Athens, Malaysia, Fiji, Mongolia, Arizona, Peru. He passes them to Rahim and Amy. There's an old map of the world that's been folded, torn, and then mended with adhesive tape. Every place he visited is marked with annotations. Next to London, he sees the letters "JP." Marc had diligently followed every step of Jean-Philippe's journey on behalf of the *World Compass*.

At the bottom of the box, he discovers an envelope containing all his articles, meticulously cut out and arranged in chronological order. On the cover, Marc had affixed the photograph of the 'Dancing Explorer', the same picture that Jean-Philippe had hung on the wall of his apartment. For two months, his father had requested that he share each story, even though he'd already read them all beforehand.

As Amy reacts to each article, memories of their travels come flooding back, and she vividly recounts the details and twists and turns relating to their reporting. She shares these anecdotes with Rahim, who bursts into hearty laughter. Immersed in nostalgia, Jean-Philippe joins in the laughter. Though deeply moved, he doesn't shed tears but instead finds solace and joy in reliving those moments with his friends.

At the very bottom of the box, he spots a familiar book: *Around the World in Eighty Days* by Jules Verne. It's the same book that his father had lovingly read to him more than twenty years ago, with its burgundy cover and the title elegantly printed in gilt. As he holds the book, the nostalgic scent of its pages transports him back to his eight-year-old self.

When he opens the novel, his heart swells as he reads the inscription written in his father's hand: "My son, it is now your turn to take people on a journey. I love you. Your father, Marc."

Jean-Philippe closes his eyes for a moment, and he opens the door to his room. The pristine floor gleams, just as it did in the early days. Even the walls have been meticulously restored to their original appearance. He reaches for the chain to turn on the lightbulb in the wardrobe. The chest is missing. In its place, he positions the new cardboard box, bathed in the rays of sunlight streaming in through the basement window.

To: <u>Marc Genest</u>

Hi Dad,

I know you don't have an email because you prefer paper letters! But since I have a hard head, I will still continue my email message, which will remain in the outbox anyway…

I'm dedicating my new column to you. Wherever you are, I know you can read it. It's our story. Yours and mine, the one that ensures that we'll always stay connected.

I'm following in the footsteps of the great writers, putting my ideas, emotions, and our shared story on paper, so it can become immortal. With a touch of magic, our history will be etched into the earth, and it will become a legend.

I love you,

Your son, JP

The Mythographers

CONTINENTAL DRIFT

By Jean-Philippe Genest
Photographs by Amy Cromarty

The geologist explores the earth like a reader browses a book. He deciphers the stones like words. He observes the reliefs like pages. For him, movements and phenomena are artworks. He is moved by the sight of an explosive volcano and alarmed by a disappearing glacier.

The earth's crust transforms and deforms like a growing child. It crumbles and wrinkles like an old man's skin. It is shaped by the winds and the force of the waterways. The geologist remains confident: the planet lives and never dies. For generations, people have told their lives through myths and legends. The earth shines like this, even in the darkest corners.

The lithosphere is made up of moving plates. Some collide and create mountain ranges, while others slide. This is known as plate tectonics. The continents of Europe and North America are diverging, that is to say, they are moving away from each other, a little more each year. The North American Plate to the west and the Eurasian Plate to the east are moving apart by two to three centimeters each year, expanding the Atlantic Ocean. If he had traveled today, Christopher Columbus would have needed a few more minutes before reaching America! On the chronological scale of our planet, this may seem insignificant. However, the faults found everywhere on the planet are witnesses to the movements of the earth.

In Iceland, there is a remarkable place in Thingvellir National Park where you can walk between two tectonic plates. Located close to Reykjavik, the capital city, the fault is located between two cliffs—one American and the other European. The experience of walking between the two continents, one foot on each of them, is truly unforgettable. For more daring visitors, I recommend you dive into the Silfra fault, whose crystal clear water allows you to descend ten to twenty meters under the sea, and to swim between the two continents.

The myth of the continents

In the heart of a distant village, a fair and honest clan leader had a vision of a prosperous and flourishing city. One day, he met a sweet magician with whom he fell madly in love. She gave birth to two boys who became the pride of the community.

From generation to generation, the traditions of the clan were taught to allow the heirs to take over. The first son, tall and strong, became the guardian of the tribe, responsible for the rules and laws. The second son, cleverer and more curious, wanted to explore the world. He opposed the customs that he called into question, wishing to reform them by proposing modern ideas.

One day, an argument broke out between the father and his youngest son, a quarrel steeped in misunderstandings and misperceptions, opposing tradition and the avant-garde. Each accused the other of disingenuousness. What the son saw as curiosity, the father saw as impertinence. The two generations shared opposing views of life and their relationships suffered. The son, bitter about the conflicts, moved to another country, far from his village. Growing rage and resentment made reconciliation more and more difficult, with each blaming the other.

Unable to bear the hostilities any longer, Mother Earth broke into pieces, at the time that men call " The Great Tremor." His bitterness and resentment were felt everywhere on the planet. Mother Earth drove a wedge between the two men, pushing them away from each other to maintain peace. The magician used all her powers to avoid drifting, in vain. The abyss filled with tears.

A few years later, upon learning of his father's illness, the son, filled with remorse, returned to him to calm the rivalry. He built a bridge to cross the sea. The two men, no longer able to bear the distance, spoke to each other with humility in order to restore the strength of the clan.

During the night, the father died. Overwhelmed with grief and pain, the son began to run long kilometers eastward, across time zones. Running at full speed across the globe, he crossed the International Date Line to gain one more day with his father. During his last hours, the clan chief recognized in his son a man of strong sensitivity, upright and proud in the face of adversity. His son promised to carry the torch of his clan and to communicate his representation of the world, ideas that he shares with his father: the importance of respect and harmony of humans on Earth, an unparalleled sense of community. The time was no longer for differences, but for united visions.

The invention of parliament

Near Thingvellir is the oldest parliament in the world, the Althing. Founded in 930 CE, Icelandic leaders met there to decide on laws and the justice system. It was also an annual occasion to gather and celebrate.

The oldest place to parley is located on the fault line demarcating Europe from North America. Located in the center of the country, the Thingvellir Rift is the symbol of separation, and the Althing, the representation of unification. So, to prevent the country from moving away, it is better to discuss and agree, otherwise the earth will take care of moving them away.

I like the idea of walking into the rift as an analogy of human relationships. Our values are always questioned. Conflicts are inevitable, but never at the cost of excluding the other. Let's have the courage to enter the gap to understand it better. The continents are moving, and drifting is easy. The solutions to get closer are the responsibility of the people of Earth.

For my father

This Mythographers column is the first since the death of my father. A great lover of travel and adventure, he sets out now to conquer a new realm. I dedicate this column to him, a great fan of my travels. May death now be the only fault that separates us. I love you, Dad.

The World Compass, November 2010

EPILOGUE

October 2010

Rahim and Jean-Philippe arrive at their new house, located south of the Thames. Their friend Samuel searched for twelve weeks to find them the ideal residence. After a few visits, their choice fell on a residence that was unanimously appreciated, blending with rustic charm and with modern amenities. By mutual agreement, they decided to keep Rahim's condo on Canary Wharf to facilitate their weekday commute to work, if necessary.

Rahim places the key in Jean-Philippe's palm, and he inserts it into the lock. Jean-Philippe then takes Rahim's hand as they walk through the door. Since their return from Quebec, they have been inseparable. Even when Jean-Philippe is away for work assignments, they text each other every day without fail, regardless of the time zone they're in. Their reunions are always marked by passionate nights, a new tradition.

In the hall, Rahim holds his lover in front of him, wrapping his arms around him, allowing him to whisper in his ear.

"Welcome to your new home, Babe!"

"Welcome to *our* home!" corrects Jean-Philippe.

Rahim kisses his neck as they walk toward the kitchen and continue on to the dining room. Large windows provide sparkling natural light. The glass wall opens with a motorized mechanism, granting access to a vast terrace, a garden, and a small, wooded area.

"I have the impression that we're going to have fun inaugurating all the rooms in the house," Jean-Philippe says.

"I believe the exterior will offer several possibilities too. There's a wooded area just waiting for your buttocks," Rahim says with a playful grin.

"The woods or you?" Jean-Philippe teases.

Rahim laughs, hugging Jean-Philippe tightly against him.

"Do you think it would be better for me to set up my office in the family room on the ground floor or to convert a bedroom upstairs to accommodate it?"

"You go where you're most comfortable. Babe, this is your workspace. I want you to feel good there. For my part, I'll use the small studio. I don't need a very big space, and it's easier for me to put it in order."

"So, I'm going to set up my office opposite yours, on the ground floor. We'll be near each other."

"And when it gets messy, we'll just have to close the door," Rahim says, followed by a burst of laughter.

Amy arrives at the same time, accompanied by her new partner, Henry, a recently divorced firefighter. She admires his physical prowess and stamina, and he's a kind, honest man too. Jean-Philippe notices Amy's joyful expression, which radiates her happiness.

"Which is our room?" Amy asks.

"The farthest from ours," Jean-Philippe replies.

The friends embrace warmly, very happy to see one another. Henry extends his hand to Rahim, and the four of them explore the house for design ideas. Jean-Philippe and Rahim plan furniture purchases and contemplate the ambiance they wish to create in every room. Even Amy puts in her two cents. They decide to enlist a designer to offer suggestions on color, fabrics, and upholstery.

"I still want to have my say. There's no question of having any mustard yellow or fuchsia pink!" Jean-Philippe protests.

"Do you know who you remind me of? Your father. You're just like him! We'll let the decorator do her work, and then we'll comment," Rahim says.

Mr. and Mrs. Strand offered them the new house as a gift for their civil union, which they'll make official next June. Rahim proposed to Jean-Philippe upon his return from Sri Lanka, following a week of restlessness. Kneeling on the floor, naked, Rahim took out a box containing a pink-and-yellow gold bangle from the bedside table to make his request. Jean-Philippe accepted without hesitation before they resumed their loving play, marked by sensuality and erotic games.

Amy offered to be the official photographer. No question of hiring another photographer, she said, so proud for her friend. Michelle, Felix, Julie, and the children have confirmed their presence at the event. Michelle plans to arrive a few weeks early to help with preparations and meet Rahim's parents. Several members of Veda's family will travel from India to join the festivities. This is likely to be a great reception.

At a family dinner, Thomas and Veda gives the couple their blessing. Every time Rahim talks about Jean-Philippe, Veda sees sparks in his eyes, absent for too long. She joyfully anticipates meeting Michelle, the mother of a man she can now call her son.

In front of the glass doors that open onto the large courtyard, Jean-Philippe and Rahim embrace in the room that will serve as a living room.

"All we're missing are two dogs that will run everywhere!" Rahim said.

"Two Corgis, like Queen Elizabeth's!"

"Why not?" he replies with a broad smile.

"And we're going to name them Ulysses and Achilles, like the Greek heroes," explains Jean-Philippe.

"That suits me perfectly!"

Rahim kisses Jean-Philippe gently.

"Are you happy?" Rahim asks.

"More than I would have imagined. The only thing missing is my dad. I would have liked him to be present at our ceremony," he confesses.

"He will be, I promise you. We'll organize something original to feel his presence. We'll find an idea, I'm sure," Rahim reassures Jean-Philippe. "Especially since he offered me his blessing, if one day we managed to get married. I told him about all the love I had for you, and he promised to be present during the ceremony, in one form or another."

Jean-Philippe nestles in the arms of his future husband. "I love you deeply, Rahim, and I agree to spend the rest of my life with you. This is what I wish from the bottom of my heart," he declares before sharing another kiss with Rahim.

Amy and Henry enter the living room. "So, when do we start with the painting?" Amy asks with boundless energy.

Jean-Philippe ponders for a moment. "I'm wondering where to display the 'Dancing Explorer'. I think it might fit nicely above the fireplace."

"I think it's worth thinking about, but I believe it would be better suited in your office!" Rahim insists.

"Such a buzzkill!" Jean-Philippe says with a smile.

"It's still an important piece of my collection," Amy says, defending his friend.

"Don't you all go siding with him. I still hold my veto power," Rahim adds with a mischievous smile.

The friends share a hearty laughter as they lay the house floor plan on the kitchen island, discussing various room layouts and furniture placement possibilities.

Today marks a day of celebration, an occasion to rejoice. There are no more borders, no more fault lines, and there is no more distance.

Acknowledgments

Although writing a novel is a fairly solitary exercise, I can't help but think of all the people who contributed to the creation of this work, whether by offering me their point of view, diving into the text to question myself, or simply cheering me up after an eighth rewrite.

Thanks to my muses who were my first audience and who offered me their encouragement, even when the text was in a preliminary state.

Thank you to my beta readers who believed in the words of this novel, and for giving me indications to reach a higher level of quality. Your different reactions allowed me to adjust my novel so that everyone understands my intentions.

Thanks to Danny who enlightened me about illnesses and their treatments, to Ghislain for his culinary knowledge and to John, from London, who helped me situate the environment of the characters. Thanks for giving me some credibility.

Thanks to my illustrator Mathew, an unparalleled talent who knows how to capture the emotions of a story and to translate it into an image. I am delighted that my characters can come to life under your pencil.

Thanks to my literary director Cynthia, who knew how to turn the knife in the wound in order to challenge me while calming me when certain passages moved her.

Thanks to Donna Marie for helping me correct the English version of the novel and elevate it immensely. Your talent is greatly appreciated.

Thanks to my many friends who were the inspirations for the characters in this novel. I am a better person because of you, my chosen family.

Thanks to my family, from whom I went to pick up some anecdotes from our mythology. To my mother, the best supporter a son could ask for. To my father, my hero, the one for whom I would have traveled around the world to earn one more day with.

Thanks to my husband Martin, who took on the difficult task of not being the natural cheerleader, but constantly challenging me. It gave us funny moments of discussion instead of making the grocery list. You never got angry when I tested my ideas out of nowhere, in the car or in a restaurant. I love you.

Robert Bergevin,
Saint Jacques, QC
February 2024

List of novels cited:

Verne, Jules. *Around the World in Eighty Days.* Translated by G.M. Towle, Living Books Library, 1873.

Twain, Mark. *The Adventures of Tom Sawyer.* American Publishing Company, 1884.

Homer. *The Odyssey*. Translated by S. Butler. 1900.

Lists of songs, in order of appearance in the novel:

COLDPLAY, *Viva la Vida*, Guy Berryman / Jon Buckland / Will Champion / Chris Martin, (4'04) Album: Viva la Vida or Death and All His Friends, Parlophone, 2008.

NO DOUBT*, Don't Speak*, Gwen Stefani / Eric Stefani, (4'24) Album: Tragic Kingdom, Interscope, 1996.

LAUPER, Cyndi, *Girls Just Want to Have Fun*, Robert Hazard, (3'58) Album: She's So Unusual, Portrait, 1983.

TCHAIKOVSKY, Pyotr Ilyich, *Swan Lake, Opus 2-, Act II: Scene 1*, (2'42), 1875-1876.

EURYTHMICS, *Sweet Dreams (Are Made of This)*, Annie Lennox and David A. Stewart, (3'36) Album: Sweet Dreams (Are Made of This), RCA, 1983.

SCORPIONS, *Wind of Change*, Klaus Meine, (5'13) Album: Crazy World, Mercury/Vertigo, 1990.

U2, *I Still Haven't Found What I'm Looking For*, Bono / U2, (4'37) Album: The Joshua Tree, Danesmoate House, 1986.

CAREY, Mariah, *Fantasy*, Mariah Carey / Dave Hall / Adrian Belew / Chris Frantz / Steven Stanley / Tina Weymouth, (4'04) Album: Daydream, Columbia, 1995.

ROXETTE, Joyride, Per Gessle, (4'24) Album: Joyride, EMI, 1991.

MORISSETTE, Alanis, *Ironic*, Alanis Morissette / Glen Ballard, (3'48) Album: Jagged Little Pill, Maverick / Warner Bros, 1996.

SIMON & GARFUNKEL, *Bridge Over Troubled Water*, Paul Simon, (4'55) Album: Bridge Over Troubled Water, Columbia, 1970.

BOWIE, David, *Space Oddity*, David Bowie, (5'15) Album: David Bowie (Space Oddity, Philips, 1969.

STEVENS, Cat, *Father and Son*, Yusuf Islam, (3'41) Album: Tea for the Tillerman, Island A&M, 1970.